R.M.S. Nascopie

Ship of the North

Doug Gray

The Golden Dog Press
Ottawa – Canada
1997

Canadian Cataloguing in Publication Data

Gray, Doug, 1940-
 R.M.S. Nascopie: Ship of the North

ISBN 0-919614-70-1

1. Nascopie (Steamship).
2. Hudson's Bay Company – History. L Title.

VM395.N38G73 1997   387.2'45'0971   C97-900531-0

Cover design and layout by The Gordon Creative Group of Ottawa.

Printed in Canada.

Distributed by:
 Prologue Inc.,
 1650 Lionel-Bertrand Boulevard,
 Boisbriand, Québec, Canada J7H 1N7
 Tel: (514) 434-0306 / 1-800-363-2864
 Fax: (514) 434-2627 / 1-800-361-8088

The Golden Dog Press wishes to express its appreciation to the Canada Council and the Ontario Arts Council for current and past support of its publishing programme.

Contents

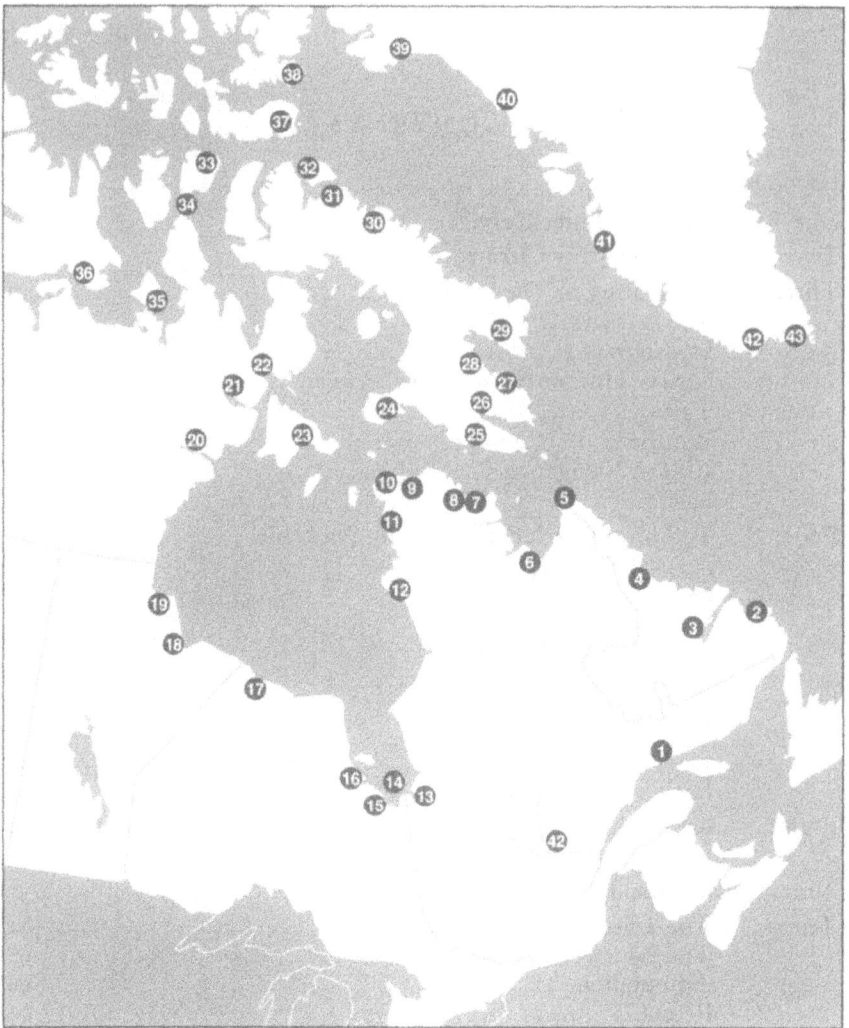

NASCOPIE's North

1. Mingan
2. Cartwright
3. Rigolet
4. Davis Inlet
5. Port Burwell
6. Fort Chimo (Kuujjuaq)
7. Wakeham Bay (Quatag)
8. Stupert Bay
9. Sugluck Inlet
10. Wolstenholme (Salluit)
11. Cape Smith (Akulivik)
12. Port Harrison (Inukjuak)
13. Rupert House
14. Charlton Island
15. Moose Factory
16. Fort Albany
17. Fort Severn
18. York Factory
19. Churchill
20. Chesterfiels Inlet
21. Wager Inlet
22. Repulse Bay
23. Coral Harbour
24. Cape Dorset
25. Lake Harbour
26. Frobisher Bay (Iqualuit)
27. Blacklead Island
28. Kekertin (Kekertaluk)
29. Pangnirtung
30. Clyde River
31. Pond Inlet
32. Arctic Bay
33. Sikinik
34. Fort Ross
35. Gjoa Haven
36. Cambridge Bay
37. Dundas Harbour (Croker Bay)
38. Craig Harbour (Grise Fjord)
39. Robertson Fjord)
40. Thule
41. Godthaab
42. Ivigtut
43. Julianehaabi
44. Port Alfred (Arvida)
(brackets signify new name)

INTRODUCTION:

R.M.S. NASCOPIE

SHIP OF THE NORTH

IN THE MARCH 1938 ISSUE of The Beaver, it was written, "Gallant, stout-hearted, patient, [NASCOPIE] is the uncrowned queen of the Arctic, and she has a history unparalleled in northern navigation. Some day her story will be written, and it will be worth reading." On July 21, 1947, NASCOPIE struck a shoal in Hudson Strait. Three months later, she slid off the rocks and sank in deep water. A half century has past without that story being written, so I decided that it is time to repair that historical oversight.

In its over 300 years of trading in North America, the Hudson's Bay Company has owned, chartered or otherwise utilized hundreds of ships and small craft. Of these, only two are really prominent in Canadian history. The first is the doughty little NONSUCH. In 1668, this 18.5 m vessel was chartered by a group of London entrepreneurs, loaded with trading goods, and sent off to Hudson's Bay to trade for furs. Aboard was M. Groselliers, of Radisson and Groselliers fame, who had persuaded the English to fund the expedition. It overwintered in the Bay and returned with enough furs to sell the backers on the idea of forming a company to exploit the trade. In 1670, King Charles II was pleased to grant the "Governor and Company of Adventurers of England Trading into Hudson's Bay" a charter and monopoly for trade with all lands draining into Hudson Bay. (The Company never got around to dropping the 's from its title.) Although these lands amounted to about 40% of what is now Canada, that did not stop HBC from ultimately expanding right across the continent. That's quite a legacy for a vessel that was smaller than many yachts afloat to-day.

The second vessel is the Royal Mail Ship NASCOPIE. Launched in 1911, this ship sailed into the North almost every summer until she foundered there in 1947. Over the years, I have read much on the North, and the name NASCOPIE cropped up time after time, either as a player in the drama, or as having brought the players on scene. No other merchant ship can boast of anywhere near such a record in waters that are so unforgiving of vessels. She endured for so long for two reasons. The first was that she was built for it.

Coming ashore

She was given the hull, power and sheer toughness to take on the ice, weather, uncharted waters and vast distances of the North. The second was that she was served by officers and crew who knew their business, knew what NASCOPIE could and couldn't do, and thus were able to get the best out of her when dealing with the risks of their enterprise.

Many hold that ships, like working animals, have personalities. Like a true pack horse, NASCOPIE carried her loads wherever she was sent, through whatever conditions she encountered, without making any fuss about how hard her masters were driving her. If there is one word to describe NASCOPIE's personality, it is resolute. When so much depended on her getting through, she battled on when lesser ships sailed by lesser men would have quit the field and often did.

In the age of steam, ships navigating the north came in three types. The least expensive were low powered vessels (Lloyd's Registry of Ships classified their power as "auxiliary"), with conventional hulls. These essentially avoided all but the lightest ice and were therefore limited in where they could go and when they could go there. The second were also low powered, but had hulls strengthened for ice navigation. These could limit damage from ice, but lacked the power to break their way through it. If they were beset, they would probably live, but that ended their progress. They could not be counted on to get where they were supposed to go, to deliver what they were supposed to deliver. Since that could be a year's supplies to the posts or a year's furs for the Company, it was of more than passing interest to the potentially out-of-luck recipients.

The third, and by far the most expensive to both build and operate, were the vessels with very heavy ice strengthening and powerful engines. These not only could survive in ice, but also force their way through it. Ice capability is, of course, a relative thing. The stronger the hull and more powerful the engines, the greater the capability. This translated into greater reliability to deliver the goods.

HBC was managed by a " parcel of upstart Scotchmen", as someone christened them in 1840, who expected each shilling to put in a full day's work, and then some. Up until 1910, they had always operated with sailing or low powered vessels, which were relatively cheap to build, operate and replace. Therefore, the question of why they decided to change to an expensive ice capable ship is a major part of the Nascopie story. She was built to carry out a number of functions under severe operating conditions. Her design reflected both the functions and conditions as her owners perceived them circa 1910 and the technology available to them in that era.

In writing Nascopie's story, I have used a variety of sources. To start with, I have drawn on some of HBC's archives. In 1955, Mr. R. Wild published an interesting biography of Captain Smellie, Nascopie's longest serving, and best-known Master, and I have used Wild's Arctic Command as a reference. Peter Newman, in his trilogy of the history of the Hudson's Bay Co., devoted one full chapter to Nascopie, the only Company vessel so honoured. I have also researched government material, particularly the Canadian Hydrographic Service's Sailing Directions and charts, for navigating conditions in the North. The material for Nascopie's sealing voyages came from a variety of publications foreworded by my Newfoundland mafia. Finally there is the Hudson's Bay Company's magazine The Beaver, now published by Canada's National History Society. Many people who crewed, voyaged in, or were otherwise involved with, Nascopie, wrote up their experiences for the magazine. They usually had a pretty good hand with a pen, and a first person story from someone actually on board generally reads better than somebody's second hand account. To the extent possible therefore, I use the story teller's own words to relate his/her tale.

Perhaps my best authority is Leonard Budgell. Len was born and raised in Rigolet in Labrador, one of the Company's oldest posts. There, he came to know both Nascopie and HBC very well. He joined the Company in 1933, and except for a stint in the army during World War II, served continuously until he retired in 1985. He served in posts in the Labrador, mainland provinces and both the eastern and western Arctic. He sailed frequently in NASCOPIE, since she was the only transport available, and dealt with her when "shiptime" came to his post. Despite the North's vast size, it only contained a small white community, and Len was on a first name basis with just about all of the players. He is also widely read on the North. Len has been kind enough to review my manuscripts, pointing out errors and adding ideas. Len also has a few stories himself to tell, and I have included some in this book. So when you come across Len:"...", you know what follows comes from a man who lived it. After discussing my third or fourth draft, I asked him, "Len, aren't you getting a little tired of my imposing on you?" His reply was that it was no imposition because he felt that I was making a serious attempt to tell the story as it really happened, neither romanticizing nor politicizing it. He also felt that, based on his vast experience and research, I was on the right track. Len's vote of confidence pretty well authenticates the book.

Over my quarter century of driving a desk for the Canadian Coast Guard, I dealt with many matters concerning navigation in the North and talked with many who had sailed there. In addition, I have been reading matters maritime for as long as I can remember. I believe that both of these pastimes give me a pretty fair background for understanding and writing the NASCOPIE story. Scholarly types may decry the lack of foot, after and end notes, but the main sources are given and "*Op cit.* Something I picked up in the Coast Guard 10 or 15 years ago" will probably not impress them anyways. While I cannot always give an exact source, there always is one somewhere. NASCOPIE's story needs no embellishment, so I wouldn't even try.

Fifty years after her loss, NASCOPIE's is still a great sea story about a great ship. She blazed her own trail in the saga of Canada's North, a trail largely ignored by all but the maritime segment of Canada's population. The North was developed, and is still largely maintained, by sea, and NASCOPIE played a critical, often lonely, and generally little known role in that development. Those truly of the North knew her role, and it is time more Canadians were made aware of it.

ONE:

Nascopie Enters Service

On December 7, 1911, the steamship Nascopie slid down the ways of Swan Hunter's yard on the Tyne River, all flags flying. Over the next month, she carried out her builder's and acceptance trials. In the first, the builder ensures himself that everything is working to specifications. Not only the present contract, but his reputation for future orders, are riding on the results. In the second, the owner satisfies himself that he is getting what he ordered. G.E. Mack, who had served in the North in the Company ship, Pelican for several years, joined as second officer. Aboard Nascopie was a crew brought over from Newfoundland who were going to take her from the builders yard round to Penarth in Wales to coal, and then across to St John's for the sealing. Mr. Mack would leave her in Penarth to travel to London to pick up more crew, mostly old Company hands, for her first trip into the North. He wrote about that year for the September 1938 issue of the Beaver. Following are some excerpts from his story.

"The Nascopie steamed well, and we went down the North Sea in great shape. The crew had considerable trouble steer-

Captain Mack

ing with the steam steering gear. They had been used to steering schooners and the hand gear of the old wooden sealers. Their style was 'hard up and hard down and steady'. ... The traffic was very heavy. We just met the colliers bound north from the Thames, and we swung and yawed like a drunken man. We passed the NEWARP amidst a blowing of whistles from indignant collier skippers who were not quite sure on which side we meant to pass. It looked at one time as if we were going to ram her. I tried my hardest to explain we were not in the ice pack, and to give her as little helm as possible. A mere second mate had to use diplomacy with that crew, who were all skippers and captains among themselves."

For Mr. Mack, this was not a particularly auspicious introduction to the Newfoundlanders he would be working with in the future. However, he collected his men in London and escorted them across the Atlantic to join the ship in St John's. This was not easy. They were sailors bound on a long voyage and, as sailors always do, had many, many friends to say good-bye to. This naturally required a glass or six with each. However, he managed to get them across in reasonable condition to sail and they joined NASCOPIE in St. John's on her return from the sealing. They then steamed up to Montreal to load for the North.

"In Montreal, the [HBC] warehouse was run by that doughty old character, Sam Galbraith. He had been with the Company forty or fifty years. ... He lived in the old McGill Street warehouse the year round, and his actual quarters were like some of the feast days in the Church of England-moveable. When his bed space was needed for supplies, Sam simply shifted it. His teapot, odd plates, and remains of meals perched on top of cases and packages. We went and loaded at Victoria pier. The cargo was stacked in various lumps for each post.

Sam was in charge of the assembling, and it was marvellous how he restored order from considerable confusion. Some of the goods were carted down from the suppliers direct: some were assembled and packed in the McGill Street warehouse.

This was the first time all the goods for the Bay had gone up in one ship. Large as the Nascopie was, we had a very full load and a tremendous deck cargo. The requisitions seemed to have been made out with a view to filling up the MAURITANIA instead of an icebreaker. [We] spent most of our time down in the holds seeing that the cargo didn't get mixed and the various posts stowed in the wrong places."

Stowage was critical. The supplies for each post had to be stowed in order of their delivery, so burlap was used to keep each post's order separate. The passengers, HBC people and missionaries, came aboard and they departed Montreal August 2.

"We called at Cartwright and Rigolet. [on the Labrador Coast]... Leaving Cartwright for Rigolet, we went round by the Dog Rocks and inside the Puppy Reef through Packs Harbour and the Horsechaps, Tub Harbour, then into Hamilton Inlet and thence to Rigolet. From there, along the northern shore of Hamilton Inlet, through Cut Throat Tickle and north to Davis Inlet, we had fog and many bergs.

We had plenty of fog after leaving Davis Inlet, and we had to go slow because of bergs. The Fur Trade Commissioner got impatient about this, and reminded us the ship did 14.2 on her trials. I explained that dodging bergs at full speed was unwise, as witness the TITANIC affair which had happened earlier that spring. Luckily in the midst of one of those conversations, we just missed ramming a berg."

The reader would require a fairly large scale chart to find some of these place names. In 1912, there were many features, particularly rocks and shoals, that were not charted at all. Some still aren't. NASCOPIE, drawing over seven metres, had to navigate these waters with neither radar nor depth sounder and deal with fog and ice bergs as well. Note also the ill-considered importuning from the Commissioner. It would not be the last time that types from shoreside thought that the North could be run as simply as their local ferry service.

At Lake Harbour, they found that the missionary "had been frozen during the winter." (I assume he only meant frost bitten. He was still alive and kicking a little.) They first had to land the supplies for both the post and the mission. As NASCOPIE then did not carry a doctor, they took him aboard until they could meet up with the Government vessel MINTO, then survey-ing at Nelson River over on the west side of the Bay.

After landing cargo and passengers at Wolstenholme, they sailed across the Bay to Churchill to do the same. The next port of call was Chesterfield Inlet, where Mr. Mack observed that

"The post had a particularly bad beach. Humping cargo on your back, in water up to the waist, was cold work till you got used to it. The NASCOPIE searchlight made a vast improvement on the PELICAN."

HBC designed canoe

The crew were invited ashore by the people for a dance, but could not spare the time. This was the story of her life over the years. In port, she had time for fun only if weather, tides or some other force prevented working cargo or sailing.

"Leaving Chesterfield Inlet, we ran into a very heavy north-easterly gale with a nasty sea about on our port beam. The sea was made worse by strong tides running. The NASCOPIE, having no bilge keels in those days and being a bit light, showed us exactly what she could do in the way of rolling. Furniture shot out and spread clothes on the deck. Pantry and galley were a continual clash of crockery, mingled with curses and tragic appeals to heaven from the cooks and stewards. Hearing a great uproar in the saloon about two one morning, I went down. The large upright medicine chest had been torn from its moorings and crashed over. Medicines, pills and what-nots were all over the floor in one gorgeous mixture, enough to cure and poison a regiment."

They found C.G.S. MINTO at Nelson Roads [a roads, or roadstead, is an anchorage off the entrance to a river and/or port], and transferred the missionary and a sick engineer to her. They then moved south to anchor at York Roads and offload cargo and people for York Factory, about 27 km up the Hayes River. The Commissioner and his party left by canoe to go up the Hayes on their way to Winnipeg, some 1,000 km inland. This almost casual mention of the canoe trip is interesting. To-day, if someone was planning a voyage like that, it would be considered a major expedition, possibly worthy of an article in National Geographic.

Eskimo kayaks off Cape Dorset

York Roads is exposed, so offloading into small craft for the long trip up to the Factory was often held up by weather. Vessels usually spent many days at anchor in the Roads, waiting for the wind to drop.

Their next port was Charlton Island in James Bay. Charlton was not a trading post but a stores depot. Supplies were landed here to be picked up by schooners and small steamers for delivery to posts around the Bay. "Miller" lived on the island year round with his family, ran the depot and served as pilot for ships calling in.

"We went over the bar with two leadsmen working, and Miller exceedingly businesslike. He could damn the man at the wheel as well as any London river pilot. We went gingerly alongside the wharf, a very rickety affair which fitted at No. 2 hatch and had a home-made railway running along it.

NASCOPIE was the longest ship that had ever been there, and we had a job mooring her astern. Wires to the wreck of the SORINE helped. One day when I was helping sling cargo down No. 2 hold, I heard a tremendous cracking and general uproar on deck. We climbed out of the hold in time to see the last stern wire parting, a couple of deadmen [mooring posts sunk into the ground] being torn out by the roots. The strong spring tide had caught the NASCOPIE's stern and the moorings could not stand the strain. The wharf gave a tremendous heave and collapsed, and the NASCOPIE swung to her anchor in mid-stream.

This meant a lot of extra work. The shore gang under Miller re-erected the wharf-a highly technical operation, but somehow they accomplished it. I had a gang putting down extra deadmen and anchors for the stern moorings for a couple of days. Then we got back to the wharf again."

Charlton Island was a popular stop because it was the only port where the ship berthed at a wharf, which made it easy for the crew to go ashore. Furthermore, it was below the tree line, and being able to walk in the woods was a welcome change.

After Charlton, the ship returned to Wolstenhome, then into Ungava Bay to run the Koksoak River up to Fort Chimo. Here they did manage some time for dancing, which could be rather strenuous the way they did it in the North. Enthusiasm was more important than finesse. From Chimo, it was back to The Labrador, putting in at Rigolet and Cartwright, before ending the voyage at St John's. She would winter there in order to prepare for the sealing.

Except for the lack of ice, particularly in the Strait, this first voyage was fairly typical of NASCOPIE's early days. She encountered a variety of problems, but managed, through improvisation and seamanship, to overcome them all. Even though she sailed from Montreal so loaded down with cargo that her marks were submerged, she got it all delivered and picked up all her returns. She lost no people, although she might well have, and suffered neither injury or damage. That she proved her design was largely made possible by the old Arctic hands on board who knew how to get the best out of her.

Eighty-four years later, it almost sounds routine, but it was never that. None of NASCOPIE's voyages were ever to be "routine", the dangers, ice, storms and interesting people made lots of variety and improvisation facts of life aboard. However, some voyages were more eventful than others. They are the ones that made up the NASCOPIE legend, so they are the ones I write about.

That legend came to be because a great ship was built, and it was manned by a crew worthy of her. Ships like NASCOPIE, tough, powerful, but expensive, only come into service where there is a particular need for their qualities. Before proceeding with her story, therefore, we must examine that need, and what was built into this ship to meet it.

Charlton Island Depot

Two:

THE COMPANY *circa* 1910

Measurement: Throughout the NASCOPIE era, the English-speaking world operated in Imperial measurement. However, as Canada has now gone metric, I have either converted measurements to that system or expressed them in both.

Exchange Rates: HBC operated in both British Sterling and Canadian dollars, depending on which country the business was being done in. For simplicity's sake, I have converted everything to $Cdn. at the then prevailing rate of exchange, which averaged $4.67 to 1 £ Sterling.

Place Names: The names used in this text are those bestowed by HBC and other white people. Many have since been restored to or replaced by Inuit terms. Eg, Fort Chimo is now Kuujjuaq. If the price of this book hasn't tapped you out, a useful accessory would be a good-sized map of Canada, such as MCR 125 from the Department of Energy, Mines and Resources. Such a map also gives the names of the various waters through which NASCOPIE and others navigated.

IN 1910, THE BRITISH EMPIRE was at its apogee. The traditional pink that showed Britain and her empire covered about 25 per cent of the earth's surface on any map of the world. The wealth and power of the island nation was almost wholly dependant on trading by sea, so over half the world's ships flew the British flag. Keeping these ships and sea lanes secure was the world-wide task of the Royal Navy, at that time the greatest of all fleets.

London was the centre of world commerce, and there the Hudson's Bay Company maintained its head office, and there its furs were sold. Traditionally, each spring, one or more Company ships would depart Britain for "the Bay", carrying that year's "outfit". An outfit was one year's supplies of every kind for all the posts as well as goods to trade for furs. From the very beginning, each outfit was given a number, so the one for 1910 was No. 240. Canada was unable to supply much in the way of finished goods, such as guns and hardware, so these came from Britain. However, as North America was able to supply the bulkiest and heaviest items, coal and flour, as well as other foodstuffs, the policy was now to ship the British-made goods to Montreal to be joined with Pennsylvania coal, western flour and other materials for the trip north. In Canada, while HBC maintained a business office and a loading shed in Montreal, the heart of its fur trade operations was in Winnipeg. From here the far-flung array of trading posts across Canada were managed by district and subdistricts managers. Each post was managed by a factor and, depending on its size, one or more clerks. In the east, HBC maintained posts on the north shore of the St. Lawrence, Labrador, Hudson Straight and Hudson and James Bays. For purposes of this book, we will largely ignore the first two, as they were usually served by a variety of local craft either owned or chartered by HBC, or other vessels carrying HBC cargo as part of their trade. The Company's "North" of 1910 consisted initially of Hudson Strait and Hudson and James Bay. Later on, the Baffin coast and islands of the High Arctic would be added.

Normally, the ship going into the North only stopped at Cartwright, Rigolet and Davis Inlet in Labrador. In the Straight, the posts she visited were at Port Burwell, Wolstenholme (opened 1909) and, after 1911, Lake Harbour. Fort Chimo lay at the bottom of Ungava Bay and Charlton Island was down in James Bay. Charlton Island was a depot. The large ships would offload cargo here and a variety of smaller craft would deliver it to posts around shallow James Bay, particularly Rupert's House and Moose Factory. On the west side of Hudson Bay were York Factory, Churchill and, after 1911, Chesterfield Inlet. From these posts, the company would also ship

Loading the bales of furs

Scottish Whaler ELIPSE at Pond Inlet, 1901

goods along the coast by small vessels and to inland posts by canoe and york boat. This system served some 20 posts in all at the time, and others would be added in future years. River transport was still carried on to some extent via the Ottawa River-Lake Timiskaming route into James Bay and from Winnipeg via the Nelson and Hayes Rivers into Hudson Bay. However, these were mainly used for mails, light freight and the more intrepid passengers. In winter, dog teams replaced the canoes.

The following example serves to emphasize why ships were required. Back in the voyageur days, forty men would depart Montreal in a fleet of canoes and paddle and portage their way 1500 km to the Lakehead, where they would land perhaps seven tons of cargo at the one port. Then they would load a few hundred weight of furs and paddle home. One hundred years later, that same number of men would load perhaps 2,500 tons into one ship and deliver it to 20 ports around the Straight and Bays in the same amount of time as the voyageurs required. Furthermore, they would deliver bulky and heavy cargo such as coal, flour, boats and lumber. For instance, each season, the Ungava ports would take up to 270 tons of cargo and the James Bay ones, including the inland posts, 1070. Each year, the ships would deliver over 1500 bags of flour, an important staple, into the North. Only ships could deliver those tonnages.

The posts had only one purpose, to trade goods to the Indians and Inuit for furs. Each post had a large hinterland in which the natives caught the fur-bearing animals, skinned them, and brought in the pelts. The post did not even receive the animals' meat, which was an important food source for the natives. For their furs, the natives received hard and soft goods and foodstuffs such as tea, tinned foods and flour. They first took some goods in the fall as advances against their winter's trapping. Then, when they brought in their skins at winter's end, they would receive the balance, as the Company figured it. While the rivers and bays provided some fish, and there were the spring and fall goose hunts, there was almost no large game, and gardening was not possible at most posts. Just as important, almost all posts were above the tree line, so there was no wood for either heat or construction, except the deadwood that floated down the rivers. Each post, therefore, required at least 25 tons of coal a year. The North was also very hard on canoes and boats, which were vital for both transport and communications. Every year, therefore, a new shipment of canoes and boats, some over 11 m long, had to be brought in. Many of these boats were the famous "Peterheads", so called because the originals were designed and built at Peterhead, Scotland. [Even into the 1960's, the Coast Guard Sealift was still humping Peterheads into the North.] In sum, the North itself supplied little to the posts for survival and nothing for trade. The ships delivered it all. The posts normally stocked for the outfit year plus one, so that if a ship could not get to them one year, they could survive until, but only until, the next.

There were also no communications, either between posts or with the south, except by water in summer and dog team in winter. As each post needed a large hinterland to be profitable, the posts were many "sleeps", as

Whaling weapons

distance was measured, apart. However, as the natives were fairly mobile in winter, they would carry letters between the posts. Back then, the HBC staff and their families had almost no other white company, excepting a few missionaries and the odd R.C.M.P. detachment. For transporting both supplies and people into and about the North, both groups hitched a ride on HBC ships, the only ride there was.

The Mounties were there as much to express sovereignty as to enforce the law. Britain had only ceded the Arctic islands to Canada in 1880, partly because they had no use for them and partly to keep the Americans out. By 1903, the hundreds of Scottish and American whaling ships that used to operate virtually unsupervised up there had pretty

Raising the flag

well slaughtered themselves out of business and departed Canadian waters. The Scots had used a pelagic system, where their ships came over in the spring, the crews hunted their own whales, and the ships returned to Dundee in the fall. The Americans, however, would hire Inuit to do their whaling and often winter over. They stocked their ships with trade goods, and, during the winter, would trade with the Inuit for meat, furs and "other services". They didn't believe in Canadian (or any other inconvenient) sovereignty, so Canada was glad to see the last of them.

Government was too busy in the south trying to make Canada more than just a geographical expression to be able to spare much in the way of resources for the North. The national railway was only 25 years old and they were still trying to populate the prairies and get regular year round ferry service to P.E.I. In 1910, 75 per cent of the Canadian population was both rural and parochial. The people's national outlook generally stopped at about their county line. How could government be spending money on some abstract concept like the Arctic when the local Post Office needed repairs? Few in the south even knew exactly what Canada was claiming in the North, much less where it was all located. Government, therefore had to

Ice boat used as ferry in Northumberland Strait

take the very long view in order to put any of its very limited resources into the North, doing just enough to keep the Americans from taking over. All Canada could afford as a permanent presence was a few Mounties with canoes and dog sleds. In 1903, Major J.D. Moodie of the Northwest Mounted Police had been appointed Acting Commissioner of the "unorganized" Northeastern Territories, and unorganized was the operative term.

In addition to the Mounties, Captain Bernier, in his tough little ship ARCTIC, was patrolling the Arctic islands, raising cairns of rock, planting flags and holding claiming ceremonies not all that different than those of Columbus, over 400 years before. While Captain Bernier was doing his patriotic duty, his crew was being more practical. After overwintering in the Arctic, they sailed south in 1911 with 1300 white fox skins, 30 blue fox, 500 seal, 350 polar bear, 250 lb. ivory and 120 pair skin boots. The Company had nothing to teach that crew. From time to time, the Government would scrape together the resources for another patrol or survey, but not very often. Its main concern was the possibility of exporting grain through the Bay, so its maritime efforts were largely limited to surveying for a terminal site and defining the navigation season for shipping through Hudson Strait and Bay. Therefore, the unspoken policy for the North was to leave most affairs, including the natives, to HBC which was at least up there and British. (Over 95 per cent of the shareholders lived in the British Isles.)

Everything the Company and everybody else did in the North depended on the ships. They delivered the goods, transported the passengers, brought the news, acted as court rooms, doctored the people, entertained them, married them and took out their furs, (politely called "the returns"), taken the past winter. The ship came only once a year, so if something was left behind one year, it couldn't arrive until the next. "Shiptime" was obviously the annual event in the life of a post, and, since the ship's schedule was tight, the three blasts of her horn as she came to anchor would bring everybody down to the beach. Cargo and people had to be brought ashore above the high water line, and other people and the vital returns brought out. Hurried visits in both directions were made and business conducted. Since landing cargo via small craft (both the ship's and whatever was available locally), was totally dependent on weather, tide and ice, activity never stopped in good conditions. As soon as everything was put ashore or brought out, steam was raised, the anchor hove up, and she got underway. The people on shore were left to sort out and pick up their goods from the beach and take them home.

HBC staff in the North normally contracted to serve for three years. For many, the Old Country, usually Scotland, didn't have too much to offer, which is why they signed on in the first place. After being away for three years, it could usually offer even less. At home, they were very small cogs in a very big wheel. In the North, they were the wheel, with Company supplied housing, food and transport. The Company would even bring in their brides, if they had lined them up. Courting by occasional mail between the North and Great Britain or the south was a slow business. If the staff could take the weather and isolation, and did not make a hash of their posting, they were fairly well set up for a career with the Company.

The fur trade was a big business. The value of the annual outfit was usually about $90,000. The value of the returns sold into the London market varied as many different furs were placed. Besides beaver, HBC also marketed badger, three kinds of bear, ermine, fisher, four kinds of fox, lynx, marten, mink, musquash, otter, raccoon, skunk, squirrel, weenrisk, wolf and wolverine. These "returns" provided a reasonable profit to HBC. In 1911, the small vessel PELICAN alone landed furs worth $147,550 on the London market (For this, her Captain earned the princely sum of $113 a month), and the total annual returns landed in London were usually in excess of $400,000.

In 1910, for the North, the Company had two ships, DISCOVERY and PELICAN, plus a mixed fleet of schooners, powered and unpowered small craft and canoes by the hundreds. One of their more interesting vessels was a 22.2 m "yacht", which gloried in the name of CHECHIRE CAT. True to its designation, it was too sensitive for northern work and was towed back to Scotland and put out to pasture shortly after NASCOPIE came into service.

DISCOVERY and PELICAN were the main units of the fleet. Each was a wooden vessel, ice-strengthened and powered by both sail and steam. [For descriptions of the major vessels mentioned in the book, see Appendix Two: Vessel Particulars.] Coal being both expensive and bulky, the idea was to sail in open water and use steam only when manoevering in ice and confined waters. The engines were of such low power that they were classed as auxiliaries. DISCOVERY was built in 1901 and sold in 1912. PELICAN was built in 1877, and as she was somewhat better in the ice than her partner, was kept in service until 1920 and finally disposed of in 1922. Neither ship was built by the Company, of course. They had originally been constructed for South Polar exploration. HBC picked them up second-hand.

However, two low powered ships were not enough to support all the Company's growing operations in the North, considering the restricted navigation season. The other vessels employed were chartered. Chartering sounds efficient because the party only has to pay for the time it uses. However, HBC service made special demands on a vessel, and those available on the general charter market were seldom built or equipped to meet all of them. The Archives are replete with queries as to whether such-and-such vessel, being considered for charter, can (or can be easily strengthened to,) withstand the ice, carry sufficient coal, carry the required cargo and passengers and not cost too much. All too often the answer was no and the search continued. The papers are also replete with tales of chartered vessels being weather or ice bound or damaged, being unable to land the cargo, cargo damaged, cargo lost, and a myriad of other complaints. Another part of the problem was that not only the vessels, but the crews as well, were not up to the task. They were used to ice-free navigation and offloading alongside sheltered wharves with stevedores to do the heavy work. Lightering cargo onto an exposed beach from an open anchorage was often beyond them. Even when expensive ice capable ships such as the sealer BEOTHIC were used, the crews could not always get the job done. Too often the supplies did not get to the people who absolutely depended on them and the furs did not get to London to pay the bills. The Company, looking to extend its network of trading posts, could not accept this lack of reliability in its supply system. The old corps of conservative directors in London (who had only gone into steam after a long battle), were being replaced by a more active set, and they decided that there had to be a better way of doing things in the light of emerging technology in the world of ships.

Bernier's Arctic off Franklin monument

Three:

Navigating the North

For some people, reading about the theory and practice of designing a ship to operate in northern conditions is as about as exiting as watching paint dry. Such people are called landlubbers, and my feelings won't be permanently hurt if they choose to do as my wife does: slide through this and the next two chapters and get on with Nascopie's tale. This is a sea story, so we marine buffs will have our day. Even with all the miracles of modern technology, navigation in the North to-day is not free of hazard. In 1910, there were no radars, radios, depth sounders, gyrocompasses, aerial ice reconnaissance, satellite navigation, accurate charts, computers, hardened steel, diesel power (even oil as fuel for steamers was in its infancy) or a collective body of ice breaking experience and ice breaker design. It was one thing to navigate in ice infested waters. It was something else to actually break through the ice without breaking your ship. In order to understand why Nascopie was designed and built as she was, therefore, it is important to understand her operational environment.

Ice

Sea ice is a complex structure with many variations, and if both the naval architect and the ship's crew did not fully understand them, their vessel was not going to get very far in the North. A chunk of ice one metre square and a half metre thick weighs about 45 kg, depending on salinity. When floating, only 10% of that chunk will show above the water's surface. A square kilometre that thick weighs one million times as much. If wind and current act on that ice, it will drift in their direction until it comes up against something, such as the shore or fast ice against which it will press until the wind and current forces change or ease. Such ice is called pressure ice, and that compressive force acts on any object caught in it. If the pressure is strong enough, slabs will ride up over each other, and form "rafted" ice, which is not only high, but deep. Over time, these slabs will consolidate into a solid mass.

Freshwater ice forms earlier and is harder than salt water ice. However, over the years, the salt leaches out and it becomes as hard as fresh ice. We don't have "multi-year" ice in the south, where all ice melts every spring and new ice forms every winter, but the Arctic is full of it.

In the south we are used to seeing ice as a uniform sheet that grows to cover the entire surface of a body of water and melts out in the spring. With its variety of ice conditions, navigation in the North was a little more complex. For one thing, the navigator did not know exactly what he was in for, as the ice regime had never been thoroughly studied. As late as 1948, there was still an ongoing debate as to whether Hudson Bay entirely froze over in winter, a factor which governed summer ice conditions. Where one year, a certain track might be relatively ice free, the next it could be covered with heavy pack.

As the navigator headed up the Labrador coast and Davis Strait, assuming the Labrador pack, up to 1.5 m thick, had dispersed, his first hazard was ice bergs. These would have calved off Greenland Glaciers and were being carried south in the Labrador current. During the navigation season, an average of 120-160 bergs per month drift down. Without radar, he had to hope that visibility was good enough that he could spot them in time. Even worse were the "growlers". These are flat slabs that have broken off from the bergs and float with only a smooth flat surface showing just above the surface. A ship could be making good speed in open water and pile right into a growler before even seeing it.

Hudson Strait drains the Bay, not only of water, but also of much of the loose ice floating around after break-up. The Strait is, therefore, a choke point and the ice, up to 1.6 m thick, gets jammed up in there and rafts, often meters high and deep, making it much more difficult to penetrate. Only in a very few years does the Straight clear entirely of ice. In addition, the

Watching NASCOPIE at work

Straight, being so far north, begins to freeze before the main part of the Bay, a factor which navigators in the Bay planning to get out before freeze-up had to keep in mind. Most of the posts were located at the mouths of rivers, and their fresh water would freeze before the salt water outside, blocking access to the post by small craft bringing in the supplies.

To the north of Hudson Bay is Foxe Basin. Being above latitude 65 degrees, multi-year ice is formed here. Further old ice drifts through Fury and Hecla Strait at the top of the basin. This ice has not only leached out much of its salt, but also has rafted, melted and reconsolidated. The ridges are both high and deep. In the spring, much of this jumble of multi-year and new ice can drift down into Hudson Bay and Strait, right across the shipping routes. Ice is always found in Foxe, even at the end of summer.

Ice navigators use the term "workable ice", i.e. conditions in which a particular vessel could navigate, so a navigator had to decide whether the ice before him was "workable" for his ship. If he got it wrong, he could either lose good steaming time by missing leads and other easy ice, or drive his ship into unworkable ice and get beset. Two things he would learn early on were, first, to always take the easy ice when he could, no matter what his power and strength. Why risk damage and waste coal trying to bull through the heavy stuff on full power making maybe two or three knots? Better to detour through easy ice and cruise along at four times the speed and half the coal consumption. Secondly, if he was in heavy ice, patience was a must. Progress was going to be slow no matter what he did and oftentimes, the best thing to do was just cut the power and wait until conditions eased. Coal was too vital to be wasted going nowhere.

For a non ice-strengthened ship, a great risk was being caught in pressure ice and being "nipped", a quaint term for being crushed by squeezing. Over the centuries, hundreds of vessels have been caught in the pack, nipped, and sank. Certain vessels such as ARCTIC were designed so that the squeezing action would force them up on top of the ice, where they would perch safely until conditions eased. For the steel icebreakers, the idea was to make their hulls strong enough to withstand the crushing forces.

Ice chunks caused by ice breaking could be carried back into the propeller and rudder, jamming them and fracturing the metal. The same could happen if a vessel was going astern in ice, if due caution was not exercised. When I was in the Coast Guard, during the sixties, an average of 10% of the vessels going into the North returned with ice damage, almost always to their propellers and rudders. Finally, if conditions were severe enough, even the most powerful ship could become beset. If her hull were strong, she would just wait until conditions eased. However, if she was beset in a moving pack, she went wherever the pack took her. That could include being dragged over shoals and into cliffs. Even the strongest hull could not take that kind of punishment without damage. There are few captains who have sailed in the North, the Labrador Front for seals or the White Sea in Russia without experiencing that helpless feeling when his ship was being carried into danger by the pack, and there was absolutely nothing he could do about it.

Bad ice and weather conditions could lead to heavy coal consumption and the possibility of running short, and there were no coaling stations in the North. Before Nascopie, ships had masts and sails which they would use in open water. However, there was always the risk of being weatherbound, which could be critical when they were trying to clear Hudson Strait before freeze-up.

There was only one wharf in the North, so almost all cargo had to landed by small craft over open beaches. The ships may have been able to work the ice but the boats could not, so shore ice could prevent the cargo being landed. Finally, poor ice conditions could so slow up the operation that the ships could not complete their rounds. Sometimes cargo could be left elsewhere and at least the essential supplies delivered by dog team over the winter. Other times the supplies had to be brought back south in the ship. Finally, when the weather turned cold, there was the risk of deck icing, when precipitation and spray would freeze on the decks and rigging. At the least, this made working on deck treacherous. Coal burners had an advantage here because coal ash applied to an icy deck greatly improved the footing. In addition, if the ice on deck became thick enough, it could destabilize the ship.

The controlling factor of the navigation season was the ice in Hudson Strait. It was generally accepted that the season ran from late July to about mid-October. More ice-capable ships could lengthen that slightly, but their real value was to be able to make maximum use of the normal season.

Hydrography

It has been said that an inaccurate chart is worse than no chart at all. With no chart, you don't know where the good water is so you proceed with caution. With an inaccurate chart, you go where the good water is supposed to be and find out too late that it isn't.

At the turn of the century, the surveying of Canadian coastal waters was the responsibility of the British Admiralty, with Canada paying 50% of the costs. However, the Admiralty had responsibilities world wide, and with the rapid growth of deep draft steamers, was hard pressed to meet all the demands on it around the world. Surveying coastal waters was slow, tedious work, involving a lot of careful sounding by hand from small craft. Canada, with its vast shorelines and growing shipping could not afford to wait for the Admiralty, so it was building its own hydrographic service. Naturally, southern waters, including the Great Lakes, had first call on its resources. In the North, its only real concern was to establish a rail-ship route to export western grain via Hudson Bay. That work consisted of selecting a location in the south-western part of the Bay for a terminal, surveying a shipping track through the Bay and Strait, and determining the limits of the navigation season. Government had no time for the other areas of the Bay, Strait, or coast of Labrador where HBC operated. There were some charts, including some local ones produced by HBC itself, but these were rudimentary. Ever polite, the Admiralty would list whole areas as "approximately charted". [Not too much has changed since. The latest (1988) Sailing Directions Labrador and Hudson Bay open many sections with reassuring words like "This area has not been surveyed..." "James Bay is generally shallow with many offshore dangers."] Much of the coast is very rugged, and the waters are dotted with hidden rocks and shoals. Furthermore, many rocks are pinnacles, rising almost vertically from the bottom and giving no warning of their presence. In 1922, the new HBC vessel BAYRUPERT was servicing the Labrador posts. On her launching the year before, she had stuck on the ways, and sailors have always considered a bad launch as a bad omen. This time, it certainly was. She was a big ship, drawing 7.3 m at the time, and her new captain, Smellie, considered her too large to work the tight waters in the approaches to the Labrador posts. On leaving Nain, he was concerned about navigation, so he took her 24 km straight out to sea before turning north. Suddenly, he went up on a shoal. Sounding around his ship, he found 36.5 m of water at the bow, 45.6 at the stern, and 6.7 m under the engine room. The vessel stayed on the rocks so her people and some supplies were able to row ashore where they were picked up after a few days. BAYRUPERT later slid off the shoal and sank.

> *Len:*"BAYRUPERT hit the Clinker Rock which was misplaced on the chart. The Hen and Chickens [which some writers state she struck] are outlying reefs from the Farmyards Island, they are partly bare at certain stages of the tide. The Clinker was well known to the BAYRUPERT pilot, Captain Harry Stone, and when they left Nain early in the morning he shaped the course to go well clear of the Clinker. He was relieved by the Captain at eight o'clock to go below for breakfast. Captain Smellie noted the course and, bearing in mind that the shoal was misplaced, he altered again but in the wrong direction and put her fair on the reef."

Just knowing a reef is mischarted may not be enough. One can as easily set a course into it as one to clear it. The records of the day are full of groundings or scrapings on uncharted or mischarted shoals and rocks, even in relatively well travelled waters. If a rock wasn't known, it was usually because nobody had hit it yet.

Some approaches to posts had the odd beacon on shore and a few buoys to mark the channel, but most did not. Even experienced captains would take local pilots when approaching certain anchorages. Some of these pilots were Inuit who were usually fine seamen. They had to be to survive northern conditions. While their craft were small, they had to know the local bottom because they fished. Few had problems making the mental leap from steering small craft to conning big ships and the captains would swear by the good ones, greeting them as old friends each shiptime. There were two legendary pilots. Navolia, of Lake Harbour was one. He, his wife, family and dogs would row out to the entrance beacon, and the lot, people, dogs and boat, would be brought aboard. Navolia would mount the bridge and pilot them in. Across the Strait was "Old Partridge", who piloted ships unerringly up the Koksoak River to Fort Chimo.

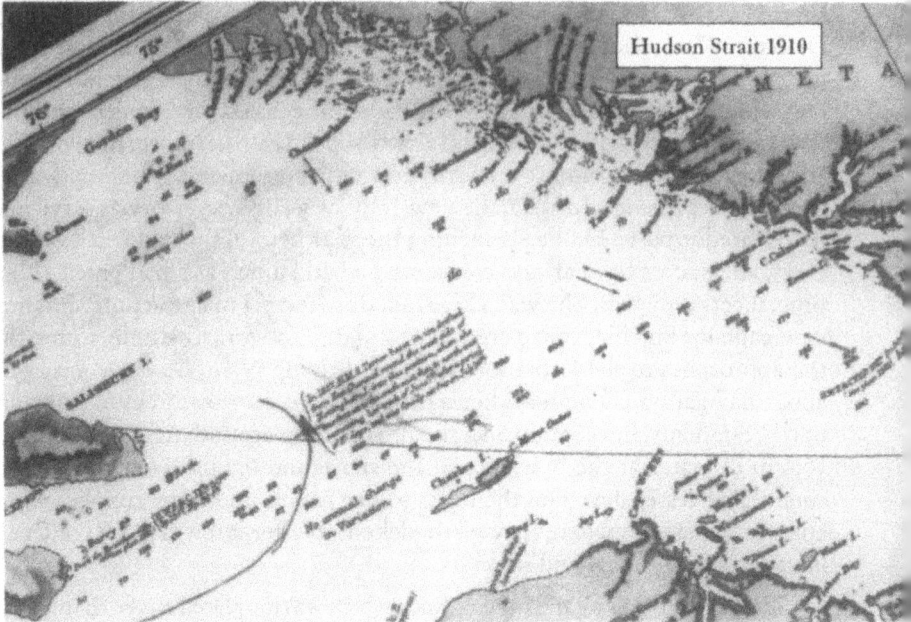

The chart from 1910 (above) represents the extent of navigation conditions known at that time. Below, is from Chart 5450, the one used today. It has the notation: *"Corrected through Notices to Mariners. Edition 11. Nov. 01 '96."* As both chart extracts have been greatly reduced in size to fit the book, a magnifying glass might be of use. There are several differences to note between the two (see page 21).

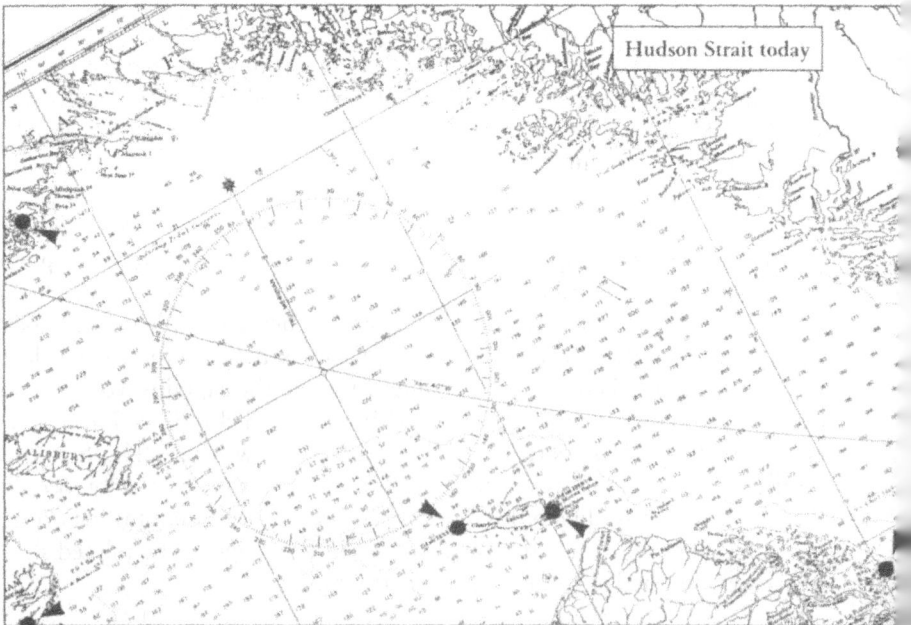

Where the bottom was soft and the tidal and river currents strong, the channel would shift over the winter. Therefore, before shiptime, the factor or pilot would go out in his boat with sounding pole or leadline and find out where the channel had got itself to. If he was enterprising, he would mark it with a few buoys. Otherwise, he took note of its new course so that he could pilot the ship in. In much of shallow James Bay, the sandy bottom was similarly mobile. Even experienced masters would lose the good water, as the number of wrecks scattered around the Bay attests.

> There are several differences between the two charts on the left.
> **Soundings (water depths):** there were no depth sounders other than lead lines back in 1910.
> **Aides to navigation:** in 1910, there were none. The modern chart shows both radio stations and shore lights at critical navigation points (see my arrows).
> **Geography:** the modern chart shows a much more accurately surveyed shoreline than the old one did, particularly along the north shore. In the 1910 chart, it almost appears that they were largely guessing about the islands at the west end of the Strait, which were not extensively visited.

Tides

"Incoming" and "outgoing" or "receding" are more suitable ways of thinking about tides on the Labrador coast and in Hudson Strait and Bay than rising and falling. Tides coming into a bay or river through narrow channels can create tremendous currents, and, coupled with a river's own flow, real maelstroms. Furthermore, depending on the geography, the change in water level inside can be much greater than that outside. These currents can make a vessel almost unmanageable. The Sailing Directions say about Labrador, "Because of the intricacies of the coastline which is infringed with innumerable inlets and small islands, currents inshore must remain a matter of local knowledge. Strong, dangerous currents up to 7 knots (12.6 k.p.h.) flow into the fiords and through the tickles [narrow straits]." In 1910, 6 knots was a reasonable speed for many steamships. For Hudson Strait, where the tide ebbs and flows between Davis Strait and Hudson Bay, the Directions quotes a 1587 navigator, John Davis. "We saw the sea falling down into the Gulf with a might overfall and roaring and with divers circular motions like whirlpools in such sort as forceable streams pass through the arches of bridges." Add some pack ice and the Strait makes quite a piece of navigation.

The tide moves through the Strait at up to 5 knots (9 k.p.h.), with a range between 10.1 and 15.2 m in height. In Hudson and James Bay, of course, the tides are much lower, although in the river mouths and narrow channels, they are still respectable. Churchill has a tidal range of 4.3-5.2 m and the tide pours through Chesterfield Inlet on the west side of the Bay at 8 knots. Captain G.E. Mack describes the approaches to Fort Chimo (now Kuujjaq) in the September 1938 Beaver. The post was 40 km up the

Koksoak River which flows into the south end of Ungava Bay. "The rise and fall of the tide is over forty feet [12.2 m] and there are three bars to get over. The sides of the Narrows are steep. The ship is literally hurled through with the incoming tide, besides going as hard as it can steam, and for a time it seems to be charging downhill." In effect, they were riding a 2,800 ton, 93.6 m long surf board up the Koksoak.

At the wharf on Charlton Island in James Bay, supplies were landed for distribution around the bay by small vessels. The wharf was a rickety affair, which regularly got demolished if the ship was careless. For all the other posts, the cargo had to be delivered to the beach by small craft. These could only beach on an incoming tide or at the top of it. Otherwise, by the time they got their cargo unloaded, they would be left high and dry until next tide. Ideally, the ship would time its arrival for low tide, and offloading would continue non-stop, day and night, as long as the tide would serve. It was cold wet work in the surf and ice.

Weather

Hudson Strait was not normally passable until at least mid to late July, so at least the ships got the best of weather on the way north, plus long hours of daylight. However, fog is prevalent on the Labrador coast, occurring up to one day in two. Particularly before radar, fog and ice, especially icebergs, made a worrisome combination. Once into the Bay, fog is not as serious. However, later on in the season, as the days get shorter, blinding heavy snows occur. When the air temperature falls below freezing, a phenomenon called sea smoke takes place. Moisture, evaporating into the cold air, condenses into a thick mist, which can hide low-lying objects.

Ships are usually on their way south before the heaviest storms appear in November, but strong winds can occur before then. Hudson and James Bays form a body of water 1,450 km long by 965 km across with an average depth of only 128 m. That type of water can quickly breed high, steep seas which even good sized ships have to respect. Fortunately, ships built for ice could take a pretty hefty pounding from storms as well. However, when moored off the posts, they did have to stand a good anchor watch, keep steam up and prepare to put out to sea to ride out the weather.

Heavy weather was the bane of cargo operations. High seas prevented the lightering craft from coming alongside the ship to take cargo, and high surf would stop them from beaching. If the weather were bad enough, small craft could not operate at all, leaving people stranded on both the ship and the shore. Vessels would haul cargo thousands of kilometres from Montreal with no problem and then be stuck at anchor for days, waiting for the weather to moderate to get the stuff the last few hundred metres to its final destination. Until the thirties, the ships' own landing craft consisted of two whale boats lashed together (called "lash-boats" naturally), with planks laid across. This cumbersome arrangement could carry several tons and was towed by the ship's launch.

Aids to Navigation

In terms of shipboard navigating gear, vessels had neither radar nor depth sounder. If the navigators had neither local knowledge nor a pilot, coastal waters could only be sailed with extreme care and diligence. Even worse, they had no gyrocompass. The magnetic compass was almost useless in the high latitudes as they were too close to the North Magnetic Pole. Even the already large variations had variations.

A ship has a speed through the water, which can be measured, and a speed over the ground, which is the water speed plus or minus the local current speed. However, if the latter is not known, which was generally the case, the ship had difficulty in fixing its position using dead reckoning, which was based on a given rate of advance from a known position.

The only buoys and beacons put out were those placed by the factor or pilot in the approaches to his post. The Government had nothing in 1910. Even in 1945, with the grain trade well established, it had only installed 12 lighted beacons in all of Hudson Strait and Bay.

Facilities

There were no coaling, supply or repair facilities in the North, not even a lumber yard. The nearest tugs were in St. John's. Fortunately, ship's plants were usually both simple and rugged. There were not that many parts, and their designs were so basic and tolerances so large, that the ship's engineer could usually get the plant back on line.

These were the navigational problems that HBC had to work with circa 1910. Even now, no captain feels confident that he/she can steam around the North at will. He/she is much better off than navigators were back then, but the elements still govern operations. The Company knew the problems. It understood that the only way that it could come close to guaranteeing an annual service to its growing number of posts, and pick up the furs on which its fortunes depended, was to invest in the best available technology for one ship. The alternative was two or more conventional ships, and ice could stop two ships as well as one. The investment would be large, but the Company would have to make it if it wanted to maintain and expand its operations in the North.

FOUR:

TECHNICAL INTERLUDE – DESIGNING NASCOPIE

At HBC's 1911 Annual General Court of Proprietors, the Governor, Lord Strathcona stated: "To put the Company's transport on a proper footing, and to avoid the necessity of chartering extra tonnage", a new type of vessel is being built. "This will assure sufficient suitable tonnage to the Company for some years to come." As usual in these things, what design that vessel was going to be came out of discussions between those who would have to operate the ship, those in the North who would be depending on her capability and reliability to make shiptime and those who would have to sign the cheques. The first two wanted a strong, tough pack horse that could handle conditions in the North. The third wanted to watch the shillings. The result was the product that slid down the ways of the Swan Hunter & Wigham Richardson, Neptune Works, Wallsend-on-Tyne, England on December 7, 1911.

For you landlubbers who have stuck with us so far, your agony is far from over. This is because we marine buffs want to know not only what design the naval architect came up with, but also how it was arrived at. His work was governed by four factors; ship's mission, operational environment, available technology and cost. In NASCOPIE's case, these were; delivering small lots (the outfits) and passengers, isolated and ice-infested, basic steel and coal-fired steam and as little as the Company could get away with paying to get the ship it needed.

A firm seeking a truck or aircraft usually figures out what it wants, then buys the model closest to that. The buyer of a trading vessel, on the other hand, works out exactly what he wants and has it designed to his specifications. The naval architect designing the vessel then has to make a set of trade-offs. For instance a large vessel can carry a great deal of cargo but her size limits the number of ports she can enter. Where NASCOPIE was going, there were no real ports, with docks, cranes and shelter, only small coves and river mouths. Moreover, even if a market for 10,000 tons of cargo had been there, the length of the season, the number of ports and the lack of unloading

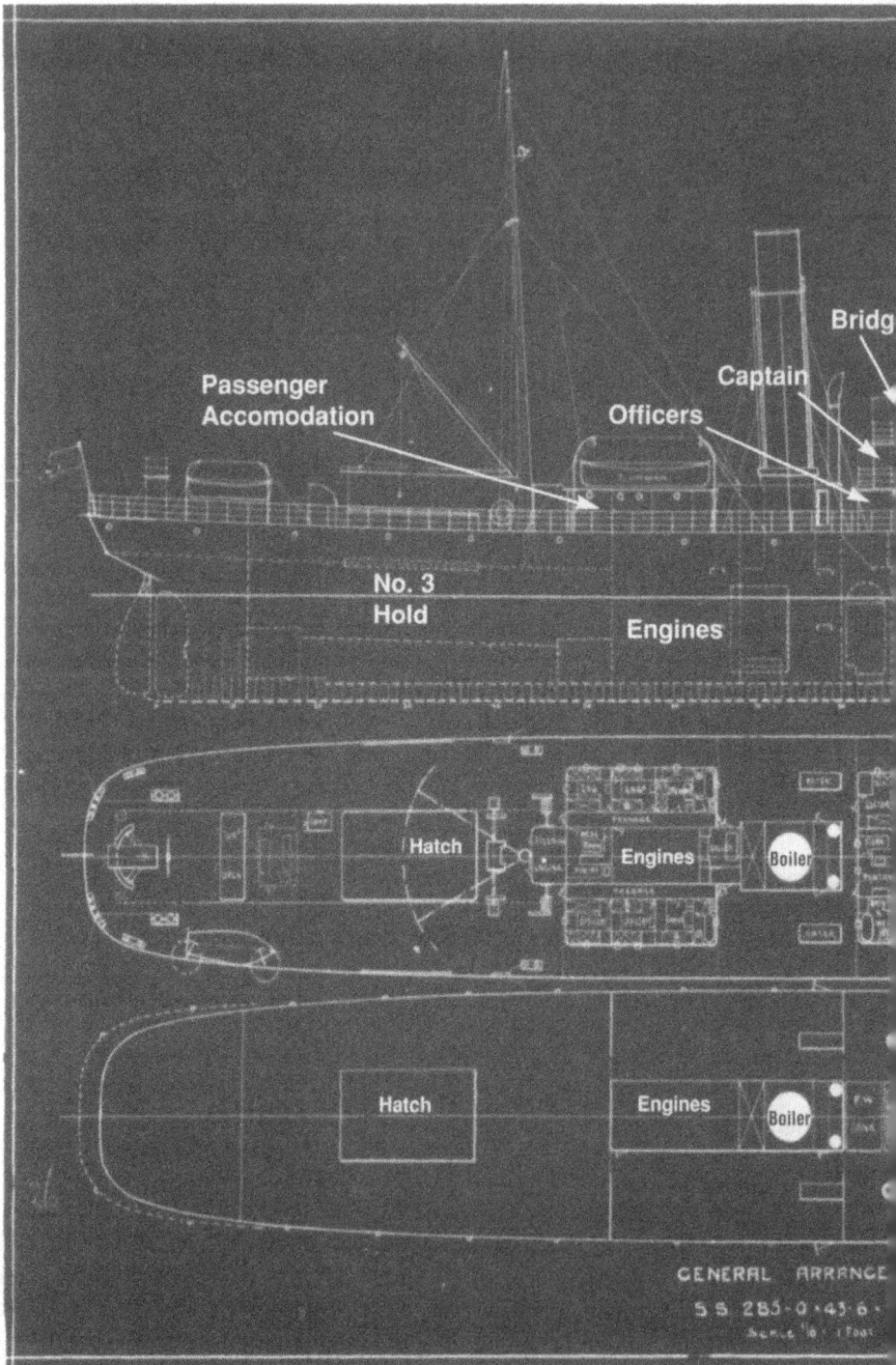

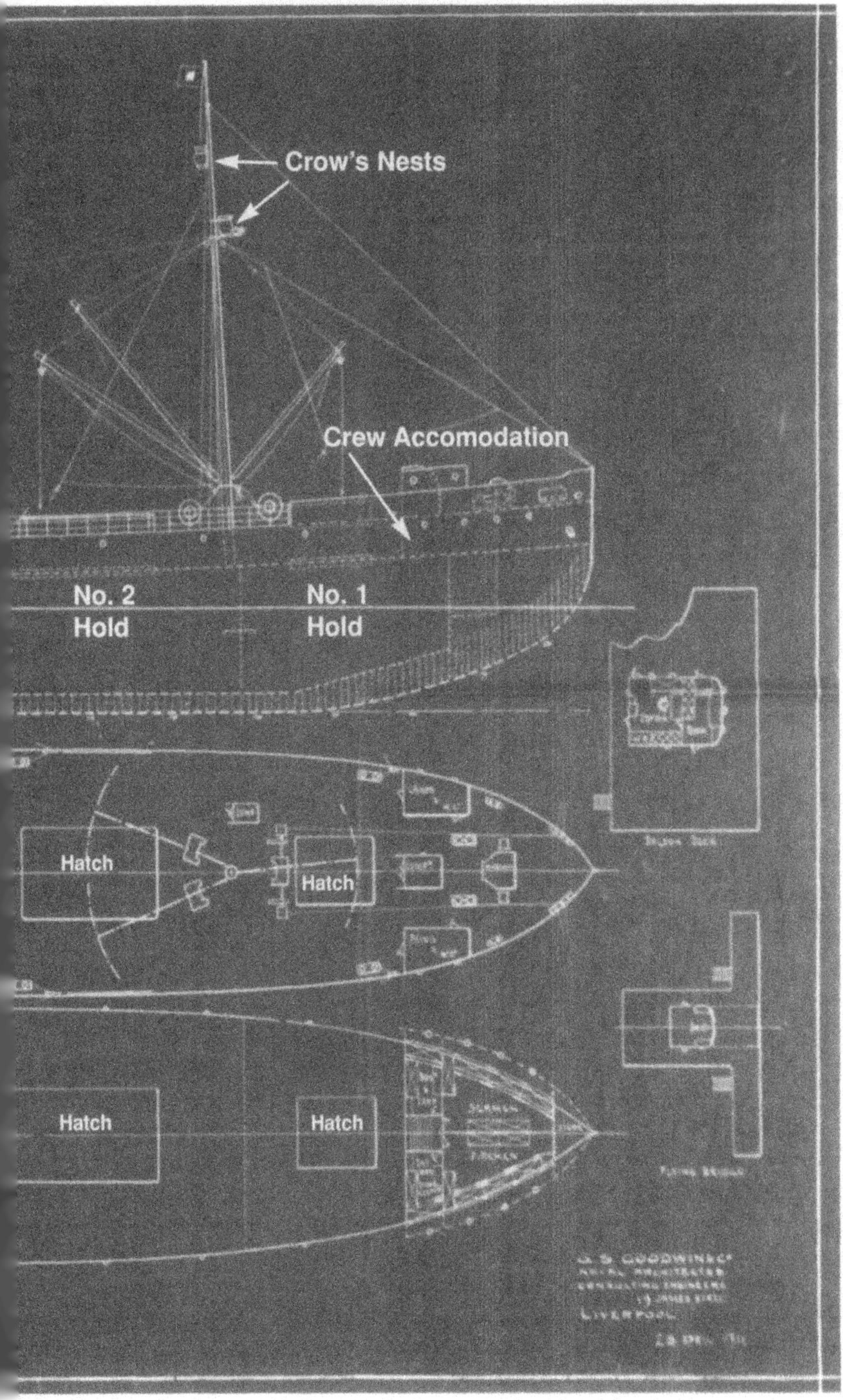
Crow's Nests
Crew Accomodation
No. 2
Hold
No. 1
Hold
Hatch
Hatch
Hatch
Hatch
LIVERPOOL

facilities would never have allowed one ship to deliver it all. That, and cost, defined her outside dimensions, including loaded draft. (Water depth is usually the limiting factor governing access to any port or anchorage.)

In addressing draft, the designer is faced with an immutable law of physics. When a vessel is placed in water, it displaces a volume of the water of a weight equal to its own. When weight is added, the vessel sinks further to increase displacement until that equilibrium is restored. (NASCOPIE's draft would increase 2.5 cm for every 36 tons added.) That additional weight can be any combination of hull strengthening, power and fuel, which allow the ship to navigate in a hostile environment, and cargo, which earns the ship money. However, a vessel can be allowed to sink only so far. It must have a minimum freeboard for sea-keeping. This was no academic requirement. In the teeth of opposition from overloading and well insured ship-owners, Samuel Plimsoll got an act though the British Parliament in 1876 requiring a load-line for each British ship. That line, the Plimsoll Line, was the ship's legal loaded draft, and was marked on its hull. In short, if the architect wanted to add steel for strength or more powerful engines or larger bunkers for range, he had to subtract weight somewhere else.

When it came to designing in ice capability, it was recognize that the most experienced ice navigators of the day were the Newfoundland sealers. The Canadian Government was trying its hand with icebreakers and there was some ice breaking being done in the Baltic and along the north Russian coast, but the sealers had been working the ice regularly for over a century, and knew how it should be done. Besides, they were "British", so they passed their expertise and requirements on to the British yards who built their ships.

While there is some real finesse in breaking ice, it consists essentially of applying brute force to a solid substance. The force comes from a heavy hull, pushed by plenty of thrust. The idea is that the ice will give way. It often doesn't and has to be hit again. And again, etc. Brute force is needed not only to break the ice but to push the hull through it. Pressure ice will continue to squeeze the sides of the hull even after the bow breaks the track. There is also friction between the hull and the ice, particularly if there is a thick snow cover. Ice friction can take the paint right off a hull, and absorb up to 50% of the ship's power. A modern icebreaker does not, therefore, have long, flat sides, but is rounded, to the extent possible, from bow to stern. It is also not long and thin, like a destroyer, but stubby, like a tug. This shape gives it, not only rounded sides, but more manoeuvrability. A destroyer may have a hull length to width ratio of eight or nine to one. An icebreaker usually has a ratio on the order of four to one. Naturally, that hull is going to take a beating in the ice, so it has to be built with great strength and hardened steel. Finally, it will have very powerful engines. However, mass affects manoeuvrability, and experience was to show that NASCOPIE's best "fighting weight" for the ice was with about a two thirds load of cargo.

The stem of a ship is the vertical member right at the bow which curves back under it. An icebreaker normally operates by thrusting its stem up on the ice. The entire weight of the forepart of the ship is thus focused on the stem which fractures the ice. The rest of the bow then widens that fracture. If the ice is ridged, the stem does not ride up but rather batters through. If the ice does not break the first time, the icebreaker backs down, works up some speed, and rams it again. Obviously the bow has to withstand a lot of punishment. (Even in the low-powered wooden sealer NEPTUNE, the bow was a mass of timber 2.4 m thick.) I came across no evidence to show that the architect addressed the question of the angle of the stem at the waterline, which is the angle at which it strikes the ice. I can only conclude that, icebreaker design being in its infancy, it was not being considered as a factor. [Even in the sixties, the concept of reducing the angle from 35 degrees from horizontal to 18 degrees was considered revolutionary.] Of course, the fact that NASCOPIE was a freighter, operating from the loaded draft of 6.6 m up to the light draft of about 5 m meant that the angle would have to be carried well up her stem, not just at her light waterline. This would reduce her length at the waterline, and therefore increasing her draft, requiring a redesign of...etc. etc. In ship design, no factor can be changed without affecting everything else. However, the keel did curve upwards towards the bow, assisting it to ride up on the the ice.

With the bow up on the ice, and the stern in the water, nothing is supporting the centre, so an icebreaker has to be strong longitudinally. The next stress she has to withstand is the crushing force pressure ice exerts on her sides. This is dealt with by strong ribs on narrow scantlings (the distance between ribs). A conventional ship has one or more keels along the bilges to dampen roll. However, in ice, these can get hung up at best and broken off at worst, so a rounded hull is required. Finally, she needs a rugged propeller and rudder to withstand the shock load when ice chunks become jammed up in them.

The trip north from Montreal up around the Bay and back was about 16,000 km. NASCOPIE could steam at cruising power in open water and light ice, but needed full power to work the heavy stuff. This would oblige her to burn more than 20 tons of coal per day. Even at anchor, she would have to keep steam on, at a cost of a few tons a day. She would require the capacity for at least 2000 tons of coal. Unlike oil, coal can be carried not only in bunkers, but loose in the holds and even bagged or piled on deck. This was not a recommended method, as coal and sea water do not go together. However, coal in the holds took up valuable cargo space and had to be shifted along to the bunkers, so large bunkers were preferred.

NASCOPIE was going to carry both a large crew and up to 20 passengers, and all these people required room and board. While people don't weigh much, they do require a lot of space, compared to cargo. Finally, NASCOPIE was not only going into the ice, but to sea as well, including "winter North Atlantic" conditions, so the designer had to factor in stability, strong hatches, pumps, lifeboats and other safety considerations. As this was before the loss of the TITANIC totally changed the legal requirements for safety equipment, NASCOPIE's gear was not extensive.

The naval architect thus had a full plate. Within a structure of limited dimensions, particularly draft, he had to design a heavy icebreaking hull, a large, heavy power plant, strengthened shaft, propeller and rudder, space for 2,000 tons of coal, accommodation for crew and passengers, and boats to land the cargo. Then, he was supposed to find room for all the supplies and trade goods required to keep over 20 posts in operation for a year. To top it all off, he had to fit two "barrels" (crow's nests) on to the foremast. From up there, her captain would be able to spot leads in the ice and pick the easiest track for her. It is little wonder that the maximum weight of cargo she ever carried was 3,500 tons of cryolite. It was an emergency shipment of that ore in wartime, when such restrictions as load-line certificates were relaxed. Conventional freighters of NASCOPIE's dimensions could carry at least twice that. However, in order to carry all that, her ideal icebreaking design had to be compromised to give her holds for cargo and accommodation for passengers. NASCOPIE's length to beam ratio was six point eight to one, much greater than the optimum for icebreakers, and included long flat sides.

In 1910, steel-making was relatively new. All the builders had available was what we now call "mild" steel. [A few years ago, a story was going around that TITANIC's owners had cut costs by building her in mild. This tale fell through when it was realized that mild was all there was.] Methods of strengthening steel, such as alloys and case-hardening, were still down the road so the only way to stiffen a piece then was to thicken it. This applied to both hull and machinery and naturally meant more weight. Welding was not available as a method of joining plates so rivetting had to be used.

What the architect finally came up with was a hull 93.6 m length-overall, breadth 14.4 m and depth (of hold) 6.6 m. Her official draft loaded was 6.6 m. and her Gross Registered Tonnage was 2520.2. Her scantlings were 31 cm for the first 30 m back and 41 cm thereafter. Her hull was of 1.7 cm steel which was doubled from the bows back to the engine room. To this was added a 2.5 cm ice belt running from above her loaded waterline to below her light line right around her hull. Finally, her stem was fitted with a heavy casing, or "ice shoe", as this took the greatest shock load. Her rudder post was 50% greater in diameter and 6.5 ton propeller 50% heavier than Lloyd's, the marine insurance firm in London who decreed such things, required. Her total displacement, important for an icebreaker, was some 2,800 tons. Lloyd's gave her an +100A1 classification. The 100A1 was their highest class, and the + denoted that she had been specially surveyed. Lloyd's believed in covering their bases when insuring a ship.

NASCOPIE's steam plant was also impressive. Six fire boxes heated two boilers, each 5 m in diameter and 3.7 m long. They produced steam at 180 pounds per square inch (psi) which worked a triple expansion engine. How much power her engine actually delivered to her shaft is open to interpretation by marine engineers. Rating of steam plants was a theoretical exercise, using a complex formula involving boiler size, steam pressure, and number and surface area of pistons. The steam could be put through a variety of engine types and the plant could be rated in nominal, registered or indicated horsepower (h.p.) NASCOPIE's plant was rated at 339 n.h.p. which apparently translated to 2300 brake h.p. In the real world, how much useful power a coal-fired plant could actually put out depended more on the expertise of the engineer and his black gang, as well as the type and quality of his coal, than on any theoretical calculation. Builder's trials are used to wring out a new vessel, both to demonstrate her capabilities and to make sure everything works. On NASCOPIE's trials in January, 1912, she went through the measured mile at 14.1 knots (25.4 k.p.h.), pretty respectable for such a heavy hull and slow turning prop (about 100 rpm). The black gang really had to put their backs into their shovels to get that performance. Some people believe that she could develop at least 2700 h.p. on her shaft when the coal was good and the Chief wanted steam, but that was never documented. Historically, a Chief Engineer without a few extra revs in his back pocket wasn't fit company for other Chief Engineers. A good captain knew that, but would only ask for it when things were getting desperate.

The vessel cost her owners $99,000. This doesn't sound like much for a whole ship, but when a good tradesman could be had for $1.00 a day, it was a fair piece of cash in 1911. Moreover, it can't be compared to to-day's shipbuilding prices, in the same way that a Stanley Steamer can't be compared to the latest iron out of Detroit.

She was called NASCOPIE, after a native tribe that lived south of Ungava Bay. Her official number, which officially made her a ship, was 129922.

Breaking the ice

Regardless of whether she ever changed name, nationality and/or owner-
ship, for the rest of her life she would officially be number 129922. On
February 7, 1912 she cast off her lines and set out for St. John's to go sealing.

Engine room maintenance

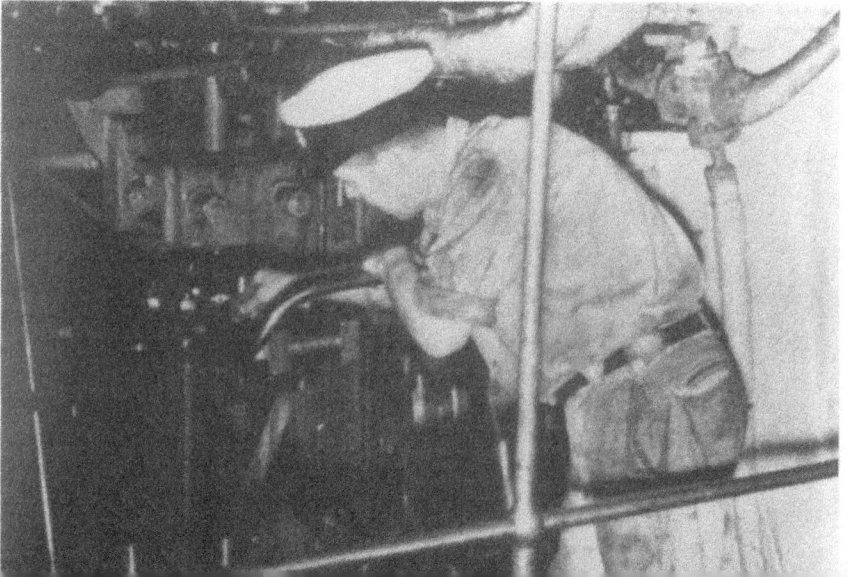

FIVE:

CONCEPT OF OPERATIONS

THIS USEFUL TERM, adopted from the military, not HBC, describes what a ship's missions are going to be and how she is going to carry them out. NASCOPIE's prime mission, of course, was resupplying the North and bringing out the returns, and that was what she was designed, built and crewed for. However, that function required less than six months per year. Except in wartime when every bottom was needed, the recurring question was always, how could she find work for the other six? NASCOPIE was an expensive ship to operate and, for her size, couldn't carry much cargo. Therefore, her ton-km. costs were always much higher than those of a conventional vessel of her capacity. She could only find work where her special capabilities were required; in the ice. If she couldn't get work in the ice, she was simply laid up until some work was found.

Over her lifetime, NASCOPIE sailed on four different types of voyages. In order of importance were her trips into the North, sealing, winter trading in northern Russia and finally, mooching up and down the eastern seaboard and the Caribbean during World War II when bottoms were desperately needed. Only the latter type did not require her ice capability.

The Crews

Because of the nature of her northern operations, NASCOPIE carried a large crew for her size. Besides navigating the ship, they had to stevedore the cargo into craft alongside, take these into the beach, and unload them. If there was construction to be done at site, they had to bring the materials ashore and then do the building. A new post would start with the store, residence and warehouse. Using precut materials, and with everybody pitching in, they could erect these buildings in three days, working as long as there was light.

Since the ship carried passengers, extra help was required in the galley, messes and cabins. There were few complaints about the food. Like any thinking manager of an isolated group, the Company knew that good food was the cheapest way to keep the people happy and productive.

While numbers varied over NASCOPIE's career, the following complement is representative of her crew in the first half of her life.

Bridge: Captain, First, Second and Third Officers.

Purser.

Deck: Bosun, Carpenter, Donkeyman (winch operator), two greasers,
      six to eight ABs (deck hands).

Galley: Chief Cook, Second Cook, two apprentices.

Messes and cabins: Chief Steward, Steward, two apprentices.

Engine Room: Chief, Second and Third Engineers, nine firemen
      and trimmers.

When radio was installed in 1913, a Radio Operator was added.

The crew not only had to be paid, but also fed and berthed. Originally,
they were mainly British, except for during the seal hunt. NASCOPIE was
crewed and fitted out entirely differently for sealing. Newfoundlanders
took the ship then. However, at first, the Newfoundlanders didn't want
to go north in summer, because that was the Labrador fishing season.
That changed over time, because the fishery was a gamble, and HBC's
guaranteed $75.00 a month started to look pretty good. The Company liked
the Islanders. They were at home in the ice and northern conditions. They
were used to hard work at sea and came cheaper than Canadians. For a
while, there were not enough trained engineers from Newfoundland, but
that soon changed. One of the main reasons that NASCOPIE always stayed
in British registry, St. John's or London, was that pay could be kept on
British Board of Trade pay scale, which was lower than Canada's. At that
time, Newfoundland was still a British colony, so the men could be paid
British scale.

Ownership and Chartering

To build the ship, HBC entered into a agreement with Job Brothers of
St. John's and Liverpool, England. Job was a large player in the seal fishery
and this was the heyday of the steel sealer. Like NASCOPIE, the big problem
with these ships was finding work for them during the time they were not
required in the ice. Joining up with HBC was therefore a natural fit for Job,
as the ship would have another five months guaranteed work each year. A
new company, The Nascopie Steamship Co. (N.S.C.) was formed, with
HBC holding 117 shares and Job Bros. 103. In addition, Job would act as
agents for N.S.C., which would relieve HBC of having to find other work
for the ship. Any user, including both HBC and Job Bros., would charter
from N.S.C. on a monthly basis. However, in 1915, the Russians came shop-
ping for icebreakers and picked up all the steel sealers in Newfoundland.
The Russians were desperate, so it was a seller's market. They also wanted
NASCOPIE, and Job Bros. were eager to sell. However, the Company had its
own irons with the French in the Russian fire so HBC wanted, and got, the
best of both worlds. They would keep the ship for their own northern business, which was why they built her in the first place, and sell her services to
the Russians for the winter. That meant no more sealing, so HBC bought
out Job and wound up N.S.C. in December, 1915.

Sealing

Sealing had been carried out on the Labrador "Front" and in the Gulf for at least a century. By 1900, most of the sealing fleet was wooden-hulled (wooden walled, to use the the sealers' term), low-powered steamers. These could get to the edge of the pack, but lacked the power and strength to penetrate into it to get close to the seals. Of those who tried, many never emerged, with tragic consequences. Between 1863 and 1914, 38 steamers were lost to the ice. Usually, however, there was no loss of life. The crew simply collected their gear, abandoned their stricken ship and walked over the ice to the next one which took them home. The great seal disasters occurred when the hunters were left stranded on the ice, usually in severe weather, or the ship was lost at sea. For instance, on April 2, 1914, NASCOPIE received a report that 136 men from the sealer NEWFOUNDLAND had been stranded on the ice for two days because of a communications mix-up. NEWFOUNDLAND and another sealer each thought the men safely aboard the other ship. Of the 136, 78 died of exposure and the rest were picked up by several sealers. Thirty km of heavy pack ice lay between NASCOPIE and the scene so she could offer no help. Out of respect for the dead, who were their friends and relatives, all the rest of the hunters in the fleet wanted to abandon the hunt and escort the dead back to St. John's. William Coaker, founder of the new Fishermen's Protective Union, was on board NASCOPIE to observe the conditions of the hunt and her men requested that he radio permission from Job Brothers to cease sealing. True to form, they bucked the decision back to NASCOPIE's captain, who decided to continue to hunt seals. After all, both his and Job's bottom lines were tied to bringing in the pelts. However, NASCOPIE lucked out on seals and left the Front a few days behind the others. Obviously, the word "Protective" in the name of the union reflected the hunters' lot at the time.

In sealing, of course, those who drove their ships got to the herds before those who didn't, so the enterprise did not breed conservative ship handlers,

S.S. GRAND LAKE founders April, 1908. Sealers saved, seals lost

especially since virtually everyone on board worked on a share or commission basis. The hunters could walk in a ways, often by the dangerous expedient of "copying" (jumping) from one ice pan to the next, but if the seals were too far in, they were beyond reach. The answer was powerful steel icebreakers that could work well into the pack where the herds lay. The first such ship went sealing in 1906 and others soon followed. It was generally conceded amongst those who went both into the North and sealing, that the Labrador Pack was much harder on ships and men than the ice in the North. Indeed, for sealing, Nascopie installed ice beams, timbers 61 cm thick, across her holds as extra strengthening. However, she still suffered more damage sealing than she ever did in the North. In 1912, her first trip to the Front was not auspicious. One day out of St. John's, she had two of her four propeller blades sheared off. Captain Barbour decided to press on. A few hours later, she lost a third blade and was brought to a halt. Normally, to change blades, a vessel either goes into dry dock or uses divers, as the propeller is usually a few metres under the surface. However, as neither was available in the Labrador Pack, Nascopie had to rely on her own resources. First, the prop was raised clear of the water by transferring some 300 tons of coal, and several tons of other gear from aft to foreword. Being down by the bow and high at the stern is a very unstable position for a ship, so she put deadmen, (ice anchors) off the stern and ran lines out to them. She also prayed that the weather would hold because her situation was precarious. Planks were then run across the ice at her stern to make a work platform. It took three days and nights of unremitting labour on the ice to rig tackle, remove the ruined blades, and install new ones. It was one of those jobs which would have normally been considered impossible but was done simply because it had to be. Nascopie missed the cream of the hunt, but she steamed into St. John's under her own power and with seals.

"Copying" from pan to pan

That was not NASCOPIE's only brush with disaster at the Front. On March 12, 1929, the Chief Engineer logged:

"Ice rafting tremendous pressure both sides aft pressure moving aft and caught rudder, star[board] quarter block wheel... carried off the deck broken in 8 pieces. Bridge stanchions beset.

"Steering wheel split, chain drum shaft star[board] side at Engine twisted... Propeller jammed could not move engines..."

Battered but not broken, NASCOPIE worked her way clear of the pack and limped back to St. John's. While the ice on the front may have been tougher to work than that in the North, NASCOPIE was seldom without company on the sealing grounds. In the North, she was all on her own.

Between 1912 and 1929, NASCOPIE sealed sporadically, as the February-May season fitted well with her northern schedule. Sealing was very different from northern operations. For one thing, the captains who took her north never took her sealing. The sealing captains were not admired for their navigational expertise (it was pretty hard to miss the Labrador Pack), but for their ability to find, and get to, the seals. For another, instead of having 40 men on board, she sailed crammed with 250-270, almost all of which were there to hunt seals. Regulations limited her to three men for every seven registered tons, or she might have carried more. (However, the regs did not require her to carry lifeboats for 270.) She only sailed with one deck officer besides the captain, and most of the rest of the organization was built around the hunters. Her engine room complement, however, remained constant, no matter what she was doing. Running and maintaining steam plants was a specialized trade, and untrained hands from the outports couldn't do it. For the hunters, conditions aboard were pretty crude. They certainly were not allowed to sully the pristine cabins, which were kept locked. Heavy planks were laid on her decks, so the hunters' boots and bloody seals wouldn't sully her pristine decks either. Rough bunks were put together in the 'tween decks and the hunters had to supply their own bedding. As the seals were also stowed in the same holds, it became somewhat cosy down there after a while. In 1799, the Governor of Newfoundland had written;

"I must ... observe that in all the dealings I have had with the Merchants of St. John's on account of Government I have ever found them the most illiberal and rapacious body of Men I ever before met with, and for this I fear there is no remedy: a circumstance they but too well know themselves."

They still had found no remedy by 1912 and the stores for the hunters were purchased accordingly. Their grub was basic survival rations, usually little more than hard tack, tea, molasses and seal meat, cooked or raw. At least they didn't stint on quantity, the hunters could have all of this cuisine they could eat. However, a trip to the front usually only lasted four to six weeks and the hunters' share money was often the only cash they ever saw from one year to the next, so they were satisfied to get anything that kept their ribs apart.

True to form in Canada's various fisheries, the natural consequences occurred with the steel sealers. When new, more efficient, but more costly, equipment replaces old, it has to catch more product just to meet its higher expenses. It naturally follows that the increased prosecution of the fishery exhausts the resource and reduces the catch, making that fancy new equipment unprofitable. By 1900, the size of the hunt, and the number of berths for hunters was gradually declining so a berth aboard a sealer was highly prized. In 1869, 219 ships and 9,181 men had gone to the ice. When Nascopie came out in 1912, there were only 22 vessels with 4,179 men. Any businessman, captain or politician that could dispense berths was a very popular man, come sealing time.

When World War I got underway, Russia was desperate for icebreakers, so the owners of four of the steel sealers were glad to sell out at a very profitable price. Russia wrecked all four.

Job Bros. took her in 1912 and she returned with 17,057 pelts having a net value of $35,540. Of this, each of the 269 crew received $43.71. The captain had a separate, usually private, arrangement. Job Bros. took her to the ice again in 1913, when she brought back 30,129 seals. In 1914 she got 17,934, and in 1915, she returned with a mere 1,216 pelts and empty oil barrels. She didn't go sealing again until Bowerings chartered her in 1927 and 1928 and Job again in 1929 and 1930. Except for 1929, she averaged almost 20,000 pelts for those years. After the 1930 season, Nascopie never returned to the sealing grounds again.

During the hunt, instead of the nice clean cargo of supplies for the Company posts, she became full of seal, hides, meat and guts. The ship became a smelly mess, and it took a thorough cleaning job with caustic soda to make her fit again for her northern voyage. In all her trips, she only took a total of 153,000 seal, not a good showing for eight expensive trips to the ice followed by eight expensive cleaning jobs and after some trips, expensive repairs as well.

Except for wartime, therefore, her annual routine became pretty well established, if not fixed. Lay up and do maintenance, usually in Scotland, for the winter and sail for Montreal to arrive in June to start loading. In her sealing years, she would sail for St. John's in winter, seal, clean ship, and then sail up to Montreal. She would depart Montreal for the North in early or mid July and return in October. She would not stop at every post on every trip, as her schedule would vary in accordance with each year's requirements. In Montreal, she would offload whatever people and gear were due there, and then she would return to the old country.

It was a good schedule, which contributed to her long service. She could rest and repair over the winter, rather than beating around the oceans earning more wear and tear. Just like us, machinery has only so much life in it, and it was worthwhile conserving Nascopie's strength and fabric for the North, where it was almost irreplaceable. HBC may not have planned it that way, but the Company got many more almost trouble-free voyages into the North out of Nascopie than any other ship they ever used.

SIX:

MRS. WATT GOES CRUISING

By the summer of 1915, much of the world was at war. While the submarine threat did not yet extend into the western Atlantic and put Nascopie at risk, nobody on the Canadian side of the ocean knew whether she would be drawn into it somehow or other and what that would mean for the survival of the posts. While shipping was at a premium, she was about the only non-government icebreaker around. If she was lost, what could replace her? However, regardless what she would do in winter, she would continue to sail into the Bay each summer throughout the war.

For the 1915 trip, NASCOPIE carried a pair of newlyweds into the North who were going to have a profound influence on it over the years. Maud Watt, and husband Jim, were heading up to Fort Chimo where he would take up his post as Manager of the Ungava District.

Maud was born into a large and boisterous family in the Gaspé. When she was still young, the family moved up to isolated Minghan, on the rugged north shore of the Gulf. There she met Jim, a clerk at the HBC post. After some years of courting, they were married in Montreal just before joining NASCOPIE for the voyage. From then on, Maud spent most of her life in the North, even after becoming a widow. The North had toughened her, and HBC supplied a certain amount of practical support, particularly in reducing freight rates for her supplies. Her efforts on behalf of the Indians, often in the teeth of HBC indifference and opposition, would earn her the title "Angel of Hudson Bay".

Maud was a sparkling young French Canadian woman joining a world of largely dour Scots traders. However, their pomposity was no match for her vivacious sense of fun and she soon had most of them eating out of her hand. Most important of all, she treated the natives as friends, rather than serfs, in marked contrast to many of the factors and, especially, the dinosaurs in Head Office. Their opinion of the value of natives can be summed up in the scale of costs and charges for taking passage in NASCOPIE in 1913. For [white] passengers - $2.30 per day, natives - 16 cents and huskies - 15 cents. However, the natives did not complain. They, and their dogs, travelled in shelter, had plenty of their favourite dish, bully beef, to eat and unlimited gallons of hot, sweat tea. Compared to their alternative, paddling kayaks and small open "umiak" skin boats, they were quite happy to travel in NASCOPIE.

The North was full of characters, and Maud met many of them on her first trip around the Bay in NASCOPIE, which she wrote about in the March 1938 Beaver. I quote from that at length mainly because her refreshing style and impish humour makes such a delightful read. Following are her thoughts after boarding and meeting the passengers.

> "First on the passenger list comes the Company's Superintendent of Eastern Division, Mr. N.M.W.J. McKenzie. Mr. McKenzie was a real old-timer in the Company's service and had risen from the rank of carpenter to his present position.... Mr. McKenzie talked ever so many Indian languages and knew all about Indians, their ways and customs. The other passengers were women, two of them brides-to-be." [They had come over from Scotland and England, to marry HBC employees.]

When departing Montreal, she opined,

> "NASCOPIE was terribly loaded, I thought. The decks were covered with barrels, boats for the Eskimos, and canoes packed in sacking, piled so so high you had to get on the upper deck to see over the top of them."

As part of his outfit, Jim had received a boat, which he christened JEAN. He was rather proud of her, fancying himself a real sea-dog. Maud didn't like the competition, although she recognized the little craft's utility.

> "This boat, rechristened the PRICKLEY HEAT by Mr. McPhail, the boatswain, came in very useful later on.... The ship sometimes anchored over a mile from the post, and supplies were unloaded on two ship's boats lashed together and towed by a steam launch.
>
> This launch... was always breaking down, and then there was a call for PRICKLEY HEAT. My husband loved this, and at most ports of call, instead of escorting me around, he would be all grease and oil.... I took

Deck load includes launch for Mounties

Mr. Mulley into my confidence and suggested the possibility of losing the boat overboard some dark night. Mr. Mulley was horrified and said, 'What would Jimmy do if he had no boat?' I didn't quite get this point of view at the time and thought that so long as he had me he didn't need anything else."

After stopping at Port Burwell, the next port of call would logically have been Chimo, where the Watts would have debarked. However, the Superintendent, now well tamed by Maud, decided to keep them aboard for the trip around the Bay and drop them off at the end. An insightful Maud wrote: "My husband kidded himself the NASCOPIE required him and his boat, but I knew better and felt quite flattered." She was on a cruise now, and owned everybody on board. She fully intended to make the most of it.

"Soon after leaving Port Burwell, we encountered heavy ice in every direction as far as the eye could see. [This is the same Hudson Strait that NASCOPIE breezed through in 1912. The ice could never be predicted in the North based on previous voyages.] Once or twice we were held up, but only for a few hours, and not very often, for the tides are strong in Hudson Straits and the ice moves rapidly. Captain Mack now spent most of his time in the barrel at the masthead, and took advantage of every little lead of open water. When the leads were closed the ship charged the ice: backed up sometimes, and charged again. One wondered how any vessel could stand such usage: but the NASCOPIE didn't seem to mind, and after a while we got accustomed to the shock and hard knocks and didn't mind either."

As they approached Lake Harbour, they encountered the little auxiliary-powered schooner DARREL, carrying Mr. Ralph Parsons, then in charge of the Hudson Strait District. Later he was to rise to the awesome position of Fur Trade Commissioner and become a northern legend. DARREL had broken her shaft and had been drifting in the ice for ten days. NASCOPIE took her into Lake Harbour.

NASCOPIE at Port Burwell

"Rev. A.L. Fleming joined the ship here, and contributed his share to the fun and good fellowship during the remainder of the voyage. Mr. Fleming has spent years as a missionary to the Baffin Island Eskimos and could speak the language fluently. Before becoming a missionary, he had been a naval architect and, if I remember rightly, had helped design the LUSITANIA or some of the other great ships. ... A few years ago, Mr. Fleming was created first Anglican Bishop of the Arctic."

The North was full of characters who had been something or other, and often well established, before they came up. Unfortunately, the histories never seem to get around to why they dropped whatever they were doing and headed into the North.

Here Maud first met "my friends, the Eskimos". "They all appeared to be in great good humour, shook hands heartily with everyone, and then commenced to investigate the ship and cargo." Their next port was Wolstenholme and from there they entered the Bay, bound for Churchill. There, she toured the huge ruins of Fort Prince of Wales, admired the Mounties "in their scarlet and gold, all well built, fine looking men", and visited the post and mission. Mr. Patterson, manager of the Nelson River District, joined NASCOPIE as she left for Chesterfield Inlet.

While he was aboard,

"Mr. Patterson was the life and soul of the ship: nothing had the power of depressing him, and his funny stories flowed like a stream. Mr. Patterson and I played poker at odd times, and for high stakes. I lost and won cars, pianos, and jewels enough to cover the Queen of Sheba."

Somehow, the typical picture of a huffy Scots manager and the prim little wife of another doesn't seem to fit into a high stakes poker game.

"The voyage from Churchill to Chesterfield Inlet was somewhat perilous, owing to the fact that for some unknown reason the compass, like the music, just went round and round. If I remember rightly, the theory was either some great iron deposits in the neighbourhood, or the fact that we were comparatively close to the magnetic pole."

The next port was York Roads.

"The NASCOPIE was unloaded by the M.S. FORT YORK and a number of large open boats, when the weather permitted, and that was not very often. Altogether the ship was thirteen days in York Roads.... I remember one rough day when the FORT YORK careered madly around the NASCOPIE with a string of signal flags flying. Captain Mack and his officers tried to decipher the message, but the best they could make of it was, 'Do you want a nurse?' They decided it was a joke, but it turned out the FORT YORK had lost both anchors, and getting no assistance from NASCOPIE had to run ashore on a mud bank. The argument about the signal flags had not finished when we left.

We had a minor incident at York Roads. On deck we carried a large and very heavy power tug.... This tug was built for the use of York Factory. It as too heavy to be handled by the ship's derricks, and two huge baulks of timber were also carried on deck to be used as sheerlegs while hoisting the tug over the side. One day, the weather was fine and the sheerlegs were rigged up to hoist this monster over the side, but it was a difficult operation.... The [tug] was being hoisted up, and was just being lowered over the side when the sheerlegs broke. The [tug] hit the ship's side, carrying away part of the rail, and went to the bottom. No one was injured, although several of the crew had a narrow squeak."

When one ship had to carry everything for everybody, even cargo she was not equipped to handle, and land it from open anchorages, it is a wonder such accidents were not more frequent.

On the days when the weather let them go ashore, the passengers toured and socialized. Two of the ladies who had sailed north with them were marrying York Factory HBC men, so they attended their weddings and feasted well.

The next stop was Charlton Island, and after the treeless barrens further north, the wooded islands seemed almost tropical to Maud. The small steamer INENEVE, which distributed cargo from the depot to posts around James Bay, was anchored there, and the officers from both ships would get together and yarn. Maud was surprised to hear them talk of sailing all the world's seas and wondered how they ended up in the North. However, they did more than just work cargo and tell stories.

"As usual we spent a very pleasant time at Charlton, and one day the captain, engineer, Mr. Wilmot and several more of us went on a shooting expedition and picnic on another island a few miles away. I do not remember how the hunters spent the day or what they shot, but I spent a lovely day picking berries and thoroughly enjoying myself. At night, when we were ready to return, we found our boat high and dry, and had to wait several hours for the tide to rise. We built a huge fire and sat

Entering the ice

around telling stories and talking. On the ship they were getting worried at our absence, thought we had wrecked our boat, thought everything of course but the right thing. Mr. Coats, the marconi man, knew I could read Morse code, so signalled with a lamp, 'If you want any assistance light two fires.' About midnight the tide came in, the men all got wet wading out, but of course I got carried. We soon reached the ship, and in no time were tucked up comfortably in our bunks."

Obviously, two things are relevant here. First, the young Mrs. Watt was certainly both able and game. Few young ladies of the time boasted Morse code in their repertoires. Second, captains should not forget their tide tables just because they were going out on a lark.

For some reason, they had a caged polar bear on board, and on the way down the Bay to Chimo, it caused a problem.

"But one day, the bear, rather a savage customer, escaped, and the decks cleared quickly. I wish I could have seen from a secure spot how he was recaptured, but I couldn't, and just had to wait. All the men said they weren't afraid, but I don't believe them. Most of them got in a safe place just as I did. Mr. Arnold, no longer 'cupid' but a heroic figure, distinguished himself by recapturing the bear."

The Watts left the ship at Chimo to start their long and adventurous life in the North. NASCOPIE sailed for the Labrador coast and St. John's, to wait for the sealing. What with being at least nominally at war, battling the ice in Hudson Strait, rescuing a future Fur Commissioner beset off Lake Harbour, having a schooner run aground and dropping a tugboat over the side in York Roads, stranding their boat at Charlton Island and chasing a polar bear round the deck as they steamed down Hudson Bay, it made for a full trip. It was also a good introduction for the newlyweds to the rigours of the North. It was somewhat typical of NASCOPIE's trips, but unfortunately she seldom carried such a spirited and stimulating writer as Maud Watt along to record them.

S.S. INENEW at Charlton Island

SEVEN:

NASCOPIE SAILS TO RUSSIA

W AR BROKE OUT IN AUGUST, 1914, and it soon became apparent that the troops were not going to be home by Christmas. France had never owned a large merchant marine, and, when the scope of the logistics that were going to be required became recognized, she found herself desperate for bottoms. In addition, she needed to buy huge quantities of munitions and other material from North America, but lacked an agency there to organize the purchase and shipping of these stores. HBC was admirably situated to help out in both areas. It did much business in North America and was familiar with the shipping world. Its governors also had excellent connections in the French Ministry. In addition, the British government had stopped the London fur sale. For morale purposes, they could not have British youth shedding blood in the trenches of France while their "betters" paraded around Picadilly in new fur apparel. On a more practical note, it was a misuse of scarce dollars. The Company was thus stuck with no income from its fur-trading investment in the North. However, it did not want to abandon its posts, but rather sustain them to maintain its post-war presence. The end result of all this calculation and negotiation was that, in 1915, HBC signed a very large, and very

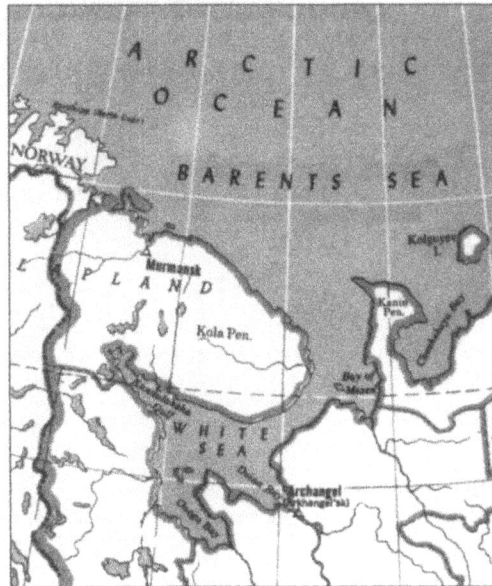

lucrative contract with the French whereby the Company would act as both France's North American purchasing agency and its agent for shipping world-wide. This contract would, during the war, make HBC one of the largest shipping firms in the world, controlling over 280 vessels of many flags. She didn't control all those vessels at the same time, however, as German submarines kept sinking them. Some 130 were lost. The contract would also produce revenues for the Company of $5,907,550 over five years. Such revenues and demands on its resources would make the Company somewhat less attentive to its business in the North than it otherwise would have been.

The French also had a commitment to supply munitions to Russia and Rumania in return for grain. Since the Germans controlled access to the Baltic and the Turks to the Black Sea, the only sea route to European Russia and the eastern front was via the Arctic. The ports of Murmansk and its sister Alexandrovsk lie on Russia's north coast. The warm Gulf Stream flows by, keeping them almost ice-free year round. However, in 1915, neither port had good communications with western Russia, although a railway connection from St. Petersburg was under construction. (About 1000 Canadians were involved in this project.) A few miles to the east lies the entrance to the White Sea, and about 800 km up its eastern shore on the Dwina River lies Archangel. This was Russia's main Arctic port with good overland connections to the south and through which she exported grain. Archangel was so important to HBC's French contract that the Company opened an office there. The White Sea is almost fresh water and not warmed by the Gulf Stream, so it freezes over early and hard. Therefore, in addition to conventional vessels, ships with ice capability were required to freight munitions from the coastal ports up to Archangel in winter. A good part of Russia's icebreaking fleet was bottled up in the Baltic so she had bought four Newfoundland steel hulled sealers, but even these were not enough. (The owners were glad to sell them at extremely lucrative prices because the declining seal hunt wasn't paying for these expensive ships.) In addition, their Russian crews did not know how to use them in ice. The Russians tried to buy NASCOPIE as well, but she was all HBC had, and they needed her for the North. Job Brothers, recognizing that the writing was on the wall for steel sealers, wanted to take the Russian cash offer, $397,000, later believed raised to $485,680, and run. However, such was Russia's desperation, and so rich the French contract, that the Company agreed to charter her to Russia for the winter. They had to get Job out of the way, so HBC bought them out for $118,187.00 and N.S.C. was wound up. The decks were clear for NASCOPIE to sail to Russia.

It was to be dirty, dangerous work. German submarines were patrolling the North, Norwegian and Barents Seas. In winter, the Arctic Pack extended to within a few hundred km of the Russian coast, limiting a vessel's freedom of movement. NASCOPIE would be packed with munitions, so one hit or a fire on board could destroy her, probably before the crew could even get off. She would not be totally defenceless, though. She was given a coat of battleship grey and a three pounder gun built in 1857 that used black powder. The fact that it was stern-mounted tells us just what her defensive tactics were supposed to be. The German High Seas Fleet may have been cowering in port, but it was not because NASCOPIE was at sea.

In peace time, shippers use their ships as productively as they can. They do not let them sit idle. They line up cargoes for them in advance and send them to ports that can handle that cargo. They keep close tabs on both their ships and their freight. In war-time, things were different. The navies took over the merchant ships and sent them to strange places carrying strange cargoes. If they were going in convoy, they had to wait for it to be formed, proceed at the speed of the slowest ships and when it arrived at its destination, queue for unloading. The Naval Control of Shipping function was not really the feather in the cap for a career minded naval officer, so it seldom got the best people. With all the muddle of war, navies tended to lose track of both ships and cargoes, and this was complicated by mandatory radio silence. Finally, when navies sent a ship somewhere, they often forgot to tell the destination that the ship was coming, and what was in it. Even worse was to be told to go some place "for orders", usually a euphemism for saying that the authorities didn't know what to do with the ship, and wanted her out of their hair until they could think of something. NASCOPIE was to suffer naval control through two wars. In both, her masters were glad to get back to the Bay, where, despite the ice, fog, storms and landing cargo over open beaches, at least there was a semblance of purpose and organization.

Captain Mack had the ship for the 1916 and 1917 trips to Russia, and he wrote about them in the December 1938 and June 1939 issues of the Beaver.

1916

NASCOPIE freighted a large cargo of dried fish to Alicante, Spain and Naples, Italy. She then sailed for Liverpool and Brest in December, 1915. After loading munitions, she departed Brest on January 3 bound for Alexandrovsk, a few km away from Murmansk. Off Iceland, she was boarded by a British cruiser who suspected her of being a German raider. Apparently, they imagined that her "barrels" would be used for spotting target ships. I guess if one was beating around off Iceland long enough in winter, one could imagine just about anything. Captain Mack describes conditions: "We had some rotten weather, and we moved in practically total darkness. It was cold, too, but these things are normal 300 miles north of the Arctic Circle in January." Once in Alexandrovsk Roads, the Captain came up against both British and Russian bureaucracy. First, the Harbourmaster, Ussekoff, came out to lead him into the harbour. Mack was assured that the approaches had been thoroughly surveyed by the man himself. Under his direction, they got underway and promptly bumped a rock that Ussekoff had missed in his "thorough" survey.

Nascopie loading at Brest 1916. Note war paint

As Nascopie was making a little water, Mack called on the local Royal Navy detachment for help. They dived on the ship and found one slightly sprung plate, so Nascopie offloaded her cargo and sailed back to Cardiff for repairs. They loaded more munitions at Cardiff and Brest and were ready to sail north again, but the Navy told them to wait, which they did, for a week. She was then ordered to Milford Haven where the authorities asked what she was there for. Three days later, she was sent to Belfast, where it happened again. Mack pointed out that they were full of munitions and anchored in the middle of one of Britain's largest and most vital shipyards, Harland & Wolf's, "and if Nascopie should blow, there would be quite a mess." That got their attention and she was hustled out of the harbour to the roads, where she swung at anchor for two more days "for orders". It finally dawned on someone that, since she was loaded with munitions for Russia, that is where she should go, and she sailed the next morning. She had wasted two weeks stooging around the British Isles in submarine waters, loaded with munitions that Russia desperately needed.

Arriving at Alexandrovsk, she found the four Newfoundland sealers, which Russia had just purchased. Two of them still had Newfoundland crews on board. The local Russian Admiral wanted the ships sailed to Archangel, but the crews refused. It was beyond their contract. The Admiral threatened to conscript them, but they threw him off their ships. A possible Russo-Newfoundland war was only averted with some tactful desk-pounding by the Royal Navy.

NASCOPIE spent the rest of the winter and spring hauling cargo between Alexandrovsk and Murmansk on the coast and Archangel up the White Sea. Often she was required to escort ships through the ice, and Captain Mack was continually put out by the incompetence of the Russian commanders. Even with a tough ex-sealer under them, they had no idea how to work the ice. One time he was escorting the Russian steamer MOGILOFF. He got her into what he considered easy ice and advised that he was going on ahead. After he had steamed about 50 km., she called him back.

> "Back we went and found her stopped. About a half-mile apart were three floes, none of which would have harboured a decent sized bear. Her skipper was prancing the bridge, resplendent in uniform and flowing cape with a dinky little dirk or toy sword. He was suffering from an attack of ice fever. The NASCOPIE went ahead at nine knots and he followed us to the bar [off the Dwina]."

Captain Mack saw not only how incompetent was the Russian officer class, but also how miserably it treated the lower classes, both military and civilian. He did not mention revolution, but, after the following story, the reader is left in little doubt why it came.

The ex-sealer ICELAND had sailed from Archangel to Murmansk carrying 160 people who were to stevedore cargo in the latter port. While downbound in the ice, she had been recalled back to Archangel.

> "On receiving the recall, the captain of the ICELAND had put these people on the ice and told them to walk to the shore. We picked them up, among them three women and two children who would have quite a job reaching the land. There was at least a mile or two of open water between the main ice and the shore. They had... practically no food, with the exception of the port side of a horse which had been skinned and frozen. Three or four men were pulling it over the ice with a rope."

NASCOPIE took them into safe haven on her own. To the Russian officers, they were simply expendable.

Perhaps NASCOPIE's finest moment occurred when she came across the French auxiliary cruiser CHAMPAGNE. On board were the Premier of France and his Minister of Munitions, returning from a meeting with their Russian counterparts. CHAMPAGNE was being escorted by ICELAND, who was making a hash of the job. CHAMPAGNE asked NASCOPIE for help.

> "The NASCOPIE was in fine trim, being just more than two-thirds loaded with timber...., and she handled well. We would come up at full speed alongside the CHAMPAGNE within a few feet of her sides. We were lucky, and never touched her. During this time, the ICELAND was laying off the starboard bow of the CHAMPAGNE at right angles to her, about a half-mile off. When we had loosened the CHAMPAGNE, I worked ahead of her, cleared the way, and went on when all seemed all right. I blew for the CHAMPAGNE to come ahead, which she started to do. This seemed to wake the ICELAND up: she went ahead and pushed a large flow right before the CHAMPAGNE and jammed her in again. All this work for nothing!"

Captain Mack wanted to leave CHAMPAGNE to ICELAND, but the French ship called him back. Then followed a conference of all three masters aboard CHAMPAGNE. It was fortunate for the Russian captain that they were in Russian waters and that the French were diplomats else they might have told him where to shove his ship. It was agreed to let NASCOPIE do the escort.

"In about thirty hours, we had the CHAMPAGNE in open water and through the ice. The captain of the CHAMPAGNE followed us like a lion. I am afraid the CHAMPAGNE leaked considerably foreword on arrival in Brest but there was no serious damage done. Before we parted, the CHAMPAGNE captain thanked us formally – I was a filthy sight, sooty and unshaven from having been in the barrel most of the time. Later, in Brest, we saw our pictures in 'L'Illustration', and were rather conceited."

BACK TO THE BAY

It was time to be getting home to prepare for the North. After a few more adventures, NASCOPIE duly arrived in Montreal, better late than never. She did not clear Montreal until August 11, 1916, when she normally would have been well into the Bay. She did the posts on the Strait and spent a day searching for a vessel reported lost. She was continually dogged by weather, which halted boat work for days at a time. At Churchill, she could not work cargo for a week, but since the post was running short of supplies, they had to be put ashore. They delivered a new launch to the R.C.M.P. at

Eskimo coming off to take passage in NASCOPIE

Lake Harbour

Chesterfield Inlet, who almost lost it when it started to drag its anchor in a gale. That gale also obliged NASCOPIE to put to sea to ride it out. They then sailed to York Roads, where 700 tons had to be offloaded and ferried up the river to the post. Heavy weather held them up again and sank one of the ferrying vessels. Risks were being taken to get the cargo ashore.

It was almost October and they still had to deliver cargo and pick up returns at Charlton Island, Wolstenholme, Lake Harbour and Fort Chimo. They had used a lot of coal battling the storms and NASCOPIE's bunkers were low. At that time of year, heavy ice can drift down from Foxe Basin and choke Hudson Strait. Captain Mack had to seriously consider that they might have to winter in the Bay. We are only left to ponder whether he preferred that option to returning to the White Sea. By now, Port Nelson had a radio of sorts, so Captain Mack radioed his situation to London. He never received a reply, so he was totally on his own. On the way to Charlton, blinding snow forced him to anchor several times so the ship did not reach the depot until October 10. A full five days and nights were required to offload the cargo. Fortunately, the depot had an emergency stock of coal, so NASCOPIE was able to load 75 tons before she headed down the Bay. Shortly after leaving Charlton, they had an engine failure and had to anchor, praying they had a spare for the damaged part. They did and were underway eight hours later. By now, new ice was forming along the shore, making landing operations difficult. However, they completed their next two stops and headed up the Koksoak to Fort Chimo, whose people had long given up hope of having shiptime that year.

> "As we rounded Whale Head and came into sight of the post, we blew the siren. The whole settlement seemed to burst into life and go mad. I could even hear the Eskimo shouting 'Omiaksuak' [big ship], as I stood on the bridge. They fired guns, and clambered around boats to launch into the water. We had arrived, even if late."

Ice was coming down the river, so everyone worked cargo day and night, sometimes breaking through the ice and getting soaked. Such was their hurry to get out that they got underway as soon as work was finished, even though the tide was against them, and the new ice made it difficult to read the river. NASCOPIE cleared the Strait November 7, the latest clearing date of her career, and headed down the Labrador coast to St. John's. Another captain from some other shipping firm might have passed up the last two or three stops in order to be sure of getting clear of the Strait before freeze-up, but not a Company man, and not NASCOPIE. As Captain Mack so aptly put it, "Outfit 246 had been delivered in the Bay."

EIGHT:

RUSSIA AGAIN

NASCOPIE SAILED FOR RUSSIA from Brest in December, 1916. On arrival at Murmansk, Captain Mack came up hard against the bureaucracy of the British Admiralty. NASCOPIE had hit a lot of bad weather on the way up and her bunkers were low. Parked safely in harbour were seven British colliers loaded down to their marks with the finest Welsh coal. However, the Navy told Mack that this hoard was reserved for the British flagship, H.M.S. GLORY, and none could be spared for NASCOPIE, which was due to sail, through heavy, coal-eating ice, to Archangel. Why GLORY, which was simply acting as a floating HQ for the Admiral, had a higher priority than a ship actually doing some work, is a question for some other historian.

NASCOPIE set off up the White Sea with very light bunkers, and got herself well jammed in the ice. Fortunately, her crew were used to the Labrador Pack, and started work with ice chisels, axes, blasting powder and occasional, but enthusiastic use of the engine telegraph. After two days and nights of this, she came free. She then managed to work her way into the little port of Yukanski, with only a ton of coal left in her bunkers. Fortunately, she found a Russian collier more accommodating than the Royal Navy out on the coast, and bunkered fully. She also found the icebreaker KANADA, formerly the Canadian Government Ship EARL GREY, which Canada had sold to Russia, and which a Russian admiral had promptly piled up on the only rock in Yukanski Harbour. The Russians were trying to pump her out without having fully sealed the fractures, so Captain Mack watched quietly as a good part of Yukanski Harbour was circulated repeatedly through KANADA's hull. (The Russians eventually got her off, and she remained in their service until 1959.)

NASCOPIE, in company with the Russian icebreaker ILYA MOREMETZ, took the British naval freighter WREXHAM up to Archangel in blizzard conditions. At the mouth of the Dwina, they were joined by the icebreaker KNIAZ PJARSKY whose captain was the first commander that Mack met in Russia who knew his icebreaking. When steaming abreast, icebreakers can

NASCOPIE beset in the White Sea

be very effective, because they relieve the pressure on each other. This the three did, and had no trouble getting close enough to port that the supplies could be offloaded onto the ice and taken in by sledge.

NASCOPIE continued to break her way back and forth hauling supplies between Murmansk and Archangel for the rest of the winter. In March, she arrived at Archangel just a few days after the ex-sealer ICELAND blew up. She had been unloading containers of sulphuric acid which were stowed over 900 tons of dynamite when fire broke out. It was extinguished and the crew, who had fled, were forced back aboard by the police. Fire broke out again, but the crew were not so lucky this time. When she blew, she took many lives with her, sank the ship in the next berth, and severely damaged two others. This was a precursor to what would happen in Halifax on December 6, when the munitions carrier Mont Blanc was rammed and caught fire. Her cargo of 200 tons of T.N.T., 2,300 tons of picric acid and 10 tons of guncotton went up, taking a good part of Halifax and Dartmouth with it.

The Tsar had resigned on March 17, but the full force of the revolution had not yet been felt in the Arctic. In Archangel, the thing seemed to blow over in a few days. The nobility disappeared, the police chief and a few others killed, and the government food store ransacked. Nascopie continued to beat up and down the White Sea until on June 14 she sailed for St. John's by way of Lerwick in the Shetland Islands, north of Scotland.

Submarine Action!

On Nascopie's first day out of Archangel, a torpedo passed about 50 m by her stern. She was still in the White Sea and so headed north with all stops out. The next day, in loose ice, a submarine was sighted. Captain Mack's describes the battle:

> "I arrived on the bridge about the same second a shot from the submarine hit the water about 200 yards short of us. All hands were signalled to their stations, and the Nascopie was turned stern on to the submarine. Collins, senior gunner, went aloft [in the barrel] for the approximate range. Our first shot was short, and its greatest effect was to thoroughly frighten my dog Spider who came along the deck, legs out straight and ears back. The submarine's second effort was closer, and the water shot up fifty yards off in the port quarter. There was a fairly solid strip of ice between us and the submarine, but around us was loose ice in which we could manoeuvre. We exchanged a few more shots. The German was working towards us, but when dodging a floe he exposed his broadside.
>
> Collins took what seemed an agonizing long time to fire, but when he did the Lord was with him. It was a shot in a million and landed fair and square on the submarine's gun mounting. The Nascopie stopped. Four more shots from Collins, and there was a big explosion. Black smoke and flame shot high in the air, and there was no more submarine. Collins deserved all the credit for it."

This story stood as gospel for many years, and I doubt that Collins had to charge his own glass in any bar around the Atlantic during that time. Unfortunately, there are two things that Collins, along with many other sub hunters over the years, tended to forget. The first is that a submarine consists of an immensely strong, cigar-shaped hull with just a light structure forming the deck and conning tower on top. It is going to take more than a few non-armour piercing rounds from an ancient three pounder to do serious damage to that hull, even though they might ding the superstructure. The second is that when a submarine on the surface is attacked, it does what it is designed to do – it "disappears". If it has a nice cloud of black smoke and ice floes to do it behind, so much the better. German records show that submarine U-28 was attacked that day in that position, and that she escaped with only superficial damage. My apologies to all old Company hands for spilling the real story.

NASCOPIE WWII armament. WWI equipment was similar

The battle must have only whetted their warrior instincts, because next day they killed a polar bear on the ice. At Lerwick, they joined a west bound convoy and put into St. John's before setting out for Montreal and the North. Captain Mack does not report any excitement on their trip to the Bay, and, on his return to Montreal, he signed off the NASCOPIE and Captain Smellie joined the ship.

NINE:

SMELLIE TAKES COMMAND

I F THE NAME NASCOPIE signifies the Company's shipping in the North, the name Smellie signifies NASCOPIE, particularly in the second half of her life. When she began to probe her way north of Hudson Strait, Smellie had the bridge. He first joined her in 1917, and stayed aboard until 1919. He commanded her again from 1922 to 1925. He resumed the bridge when she came out of lay-up in 1933 and kept her until he retired after the 1945 voyage.

Up until he joined NASCOPIE, Captain Smellie's career was that of a typical officer in the British Merchant Service before World War I. He was born in Hull, England in 1880, the son of ship's engineer. Besides its large fishing fleet, Hull was a major port for the Baltic trade. Young Thomas

Captain Smellie

Kayak race. Port Burwell

never envisaged anything but a career at sea. His parents hoped to dissuade him by taking him on a voyage in his father's ship, but it back-fired. He never got sea-sick and he loved every moment aboard. Even more important for his future, he was interested in northern navigation, and read widely on Arctic explorers. He even dreamed of reaching the North Pole. After graduating from the Hull Trinity House Navigation School in 1895, Smellie went to sea as an apprentice. He started in sail, but looking down the road, he sat for his Extra Masters ticket at age 23 and went into steam. Over the years, his work took him to various ports and adventures in the Near and Far East, Europe and both Americas. On some of his voyages, he carried strange passengers. There was, for instance, a lucrative trade transporting Spanish draft-dodgers. Ships heading for Rio would stop, by arrangement, off the port of Vigo in north-west Spain where boats full of Spaniards of draft age would be waiting. They, or their families, would pay well for passage to Rio, beyond the reach of the Spanish army. The army naturally took umbrage at seeing some of its prime recruits disappearing over the horizon, so Spain leaned on Britain and the trade was stopped after a few years. In 1906, the Russian Government was chartering ships to bring their troops home from Vladivostok after the disastrous Russo-Japanese War. Smellie was Second Officer in the HAVERSHAM GRANGE, then trading in live-stock. In Hong Kong, she was refitted as a trooper. Smellie figured she could humanely transport about 1,000 men, but the Russian officers demanded that she take 3,200. While the men stewed in their hell-hole below decks, their officers lolled in luxury in a specially-built deck house. On the long voyage to Odessa, the peasant-soldiers died like flies in the fetid holds, totally ignored by their officers.

One environment that Smellie had little experience with before joining NASCOPIE was ice. When they gave him NASCOPIE, therefore, either the Company figured he was a quick study, or more likely after three years of war, was running short of officers. Smellie had been left sick by his ship in Norfolk, Va., and then suffered an arm injury as well, so he wasn't in the fittest of shape when he joined NASCOPIE in Montreal in November of 1917.

At first sight, he was not too impressed with his new command either. She looked rather small and undistinguished alongside the large wharf in Montreal, having just finished a hard year in both Russia and the Bay. She was dirty, had cockroaches, and was on her way back to Scotland and Russia. Captain Smellie, recovering from both illness and injury, was not feeling too impressive himself. In spite of all that, NASCOPIE arrived in the White Sea in early spring.

It is interesting to note the difference between how Captains Mack and Smellie viewed their Russian counterparts as ice navigators. Mack was an old ice hand, and only met one Russian captain that he had a good word for. Smellie was new to the ice, and was impressed by their capability. It may simply have been that the revolution had brought a new bunch on board the Russian ships. Certainly, Smellie makes no mention of them parading around decks with capes and toy swords. At any rate, they taught him a lot and he learned his lessons well. He also learned a lesson about misusing equipment. The Russians had ordered an icebreaker from England with a propeller at the bow as well as the two at the stern. The idea was that the bow prop would draw water out from under the ice ahead of the ship, thus

NASCOPIE at rest

weakening its support when the bow rode over it. The theory was great but for the fact that ice rafts, and the ridges extend down as well as up. When that prop struck a ridge, it was destroyed. It would only work in flat ice, and no icebreaker can guarantee it will always have that luxury.

The revolution was in full swing when Nascopie arrived and logistics were in total chaos. Allied shipping had been delivering munitions at great effort and expense to Murmansk since war had broken out in 1914 and they had simply been dumped on the wharf. Nascopie's main task was to hump the stores on up to Archangel. The work was an exercise in futility, but nobody was prepared to admit it. She arrived back in Montreal in July and headed into the Bay once again. Fortunately for Smellie, nothing untoward happened on that trip.

On Nov. 11, 1918, Nascopie departed Montreal for her last voyage to Russia. Britain (including Canada), France and the U.S. had sent a force to take Murmansk and Archangel, in the pious hope that a show of allied steel would "see the Bolshies off." Unfortunately, the Bolshies wouldn't be seen off so easily, and action ensued. Nascopie spent the winter hauling cargoes from Murmansk up to Archangel. The allies had brought in shiploads of supplies to support both their forces and various White armies in Russia and simply dumped the stuff on the wharves at Murmansk as before. At times, up to 160,000 tons of supplies were backed up there. In winter, Nascopie and other ice capable ships were expected to haul this material up through the ice to Archangel. In Murmansk, Smellie was simply ordered to load up with whatever cargo was handiest to reach, and get underway. He knew most of the stuff he was hauling would be simply left to rot or be plundered on the docks in Archangel, but orders wuz orders. Downbound, he sailed with wounded allied soldiers for the hospital ships moored at Murmansk. Nascopie's unheated holds were not fitted for transporting troops, wounded or otherwise, in winter, and they suffered abominably. It was bloody, disheartening work, and Nascopie was glad to sail for Scotland in June. With her, she took five reporters from the allied press whom the Bolshevik government had decided were not toeing the Party Line with sufficient vigour. Smellie disguised them as crewmen and simply stared down the suspecting police who might have challenged them. After his winter in the White Sea, when Smellie stared down, lesser souls tended to hold their fire. In Scotland, Captain Smellie left Nascopie for some leave and then to take over a new ship for the Company.

Under Captain Mead, Nascopie shed her gun and war paint and resumed her peacetime routine. In the spring she would depart her wintering port on the Clyde for Montreal. There, she would load for the North and sail in early July. On completing her rounds, she would return to Montreal to offload, and then steam back to the Clyde to winter, rest and repair. Her real role in the history of the North was finally getting underway.

Ten:

The Twenties

IN TERMS OF CANADIAN development, the North, other than the potential grain route through the Bay, received the normal priority, i.e., minimal. Our usual goad, American interest, was in abeyance. The Roaring Twenties were here, and Canadians had more immediate concerns, such as playing the market, boogieing it up and hauling booze to thirsty Americans. The Company proceeded about its northern business with little attention from the south.

The philosophy of the day, both public and private, was that land and resources were there for the taking, not preserving. Tree (and water) huggers like me would have had a pretty thin time of it back then.

The big development for the Company was in response to a new fad going round the tonier salons in Europe, furs from the white fox. This cute little animal primarily inhabited Baffin Island, and the Company headed up there to fetch his hide to market. This required new posts up the Baffin coast and into Lancaster Sound, well north of Nascopie's traditional beat. The new posts would have the additional advantage of being beyond the reach of the independent traders. In their small vessels, these were trading directly with some of HBC's regular native trappers, thus cutting into HBC's almost monopolistic position. However, their little ships could not handle the ice. Furthermore, it takes capital to trade in the North, and most of the independents did not have sufficient to last out the poor years. Their efforts were still only a few pin-pricks, but they bore watching.

A site for a post required certain assets. It needed a good anchorage, sheltered from both weather and drifting ice, a shoreline where small craft could land supplies and people, a level area ashore for the buildings and a source of water. Meltwater from a glacier or iceberg would certainly do as it was the purest there was. The site did not require a supply of fur in the immediate area. The Inuit would bring their hides in from hundreds of kilometres away, once the post was in place and open for business. The whalers had had exactly the same requirements for their stations, now abandoned,

White foxes

so, in many cases, the Company simply took over their old sites. Frobisher Bay had been opened in 1914. During the twenties, posts were established at Netchilic (Pangnirtung), Kekerton and Blacklead Island in Cumberland Sound, Clyde River, Pond Inlet and Arctic Bay in Admiralty Inlet. Posts were opened, closed and moved in response to changing conditions and markets, so Nascopie never had a fixed, annual itinerary. Since Nascopie was the only vessel regularly sailing these waters, she also served other users, primarily the R.C.M.P. and the missions. Some were co-located with Company posts and others were off on their own. Over her career, Nascopie visited some 35 ports in Labrador, Hudson Strait, Hudson and James Bay, the Baffin coast and Arctic islands, and five in Greenland. None of these areas offered easy sailing. The ice, bad weather, fog, and lack of reliable charts, aids-to-navigation, communications, port facilities and sources of supply and maintenance were accepted as a cost of doing business in the North. Normal shipping lines with their normal crews would have balked at running ships that way, but HBC had been up there since 1668 and had learned a few things over the years. The posts had to be supplied and the returns shipped out. To do that in the North, the ships had to be put at risk.

Nascopie had neither the capacity nor the time to supply both the existing and the new posts, so the Company was back to where it was circa 1910. It had to obtain, by purchase or charter, more bottoms. It did both over the years. However, Nascopie remained the flagship, the only ship in the fleet with any useful ice capability, so she did the rough High Arctic work, leaving much of the Strait and Bay supply operations to the lesser vessels.

The Company was in the North to make money, and make it she did. In 1920, for instance, NASCOPIE returned with furs worth $737,240. However, just because they were making money doesn't mean they were throwing it around. In 1922, NASCOPIE was instructed that "No expense whatever is to be incurred by any department [of the ship] without London approval." They were kind enough, however, to except expenditures for emergencies and fresh provisions. Of course, since the only things to buy in the North were what NASCOPIE herself was carrying, that instruction probably did not impose too much pain on the ship. HBC also monitored how its approved pennies were spent pretty closely as well. Captain Smellie, who always thought that being at sea freed him from bureaucracy, was obliged to complete 14 different reports accounting for every body, loaf of bread and pound of coal, amongst other things, he used on a voyage.

Of course, HBC did have to consider local sensitivities to some extent. In 1923, London wanted two crewmen from Labrador reinstated, fearing that they might bad mouth the Company to other employees along that coast. Such employees, wrote London, "might feel a sense of insecurity and be led to look after personal interests instead of the Company's welfare."

Besides furs, the Company ran a few sidelines.

Len: "One might wonder why an empty ship would call at places like Rigolet and Cartwright southbound in the fall. The main reason, especially when she returned to Britain every fall, was to pick up tierces [casks] of salted salmon which found a ready sale on the continent, especially in Holland. It is interesting that these tierces bore a distinctive marking as follows:

     265 (outfit no.)
     HB
     U-1 (post no.)
     Rigolet

On the continent, the name Rigolet was taken as a brand name and was the most favoured among the buyers. Cartwright came a close second, while Chimo and more southern posts like Frenchman's Island and Blanc Sablon were not as popular, not, I might add because of the quality of the fish as taken from the water but because of the handling. At Rigolet, the trade had been handed down from father to son and nothing was lost. The newer posts had not the same tradition."

Another sideline that started up in the twenties was cruising. A few well-heeled adventurous types would be taken north and be given the grand tour. Both NASCOPIE's passenger list and cargo manifest, therefore, offered a rich melange. Anyone or anything travelling to or from the North went via the NASCOPIE for the greater part.

One of her more bothersome supplies was meat. As neither NASCOPIE nor the posts had refrigeration, meat had to be delivered "on the hoof." Once delivered, along with the necessary feed, the animals would be kept alive until the temperature dropped sufficiently that meat would keep. Hayward Hayes worked at the Port Harrison post during the twenties and

Walking the beach at Clyde River

later described handling livestock there in a neat little publication called
Them Days, published by a museum of the same name, located in beautiful
downtown Happy Valley, Labrador.

> "On the NASCOPIE, we had received a shipment of pigs and sheep. The
> sheep were put on an island until freeze up. We put the pigs in a shed. ...
> told us to look after the pigs properly they needed separate pens. This we
> did. When Mr. Steward returned, the pigs were in perfect condition."

Considering the lack of lumber in the North, keeping pigs happy obviously
had a high priority.

NASCOPIE carried, often with their families, HBC personnel,
Government officials, Mounties, missionaries, explorers and other adventurers, tourists, miscellaneous hangers-on and Inuit families complete with
dogs. She also delivered all their supplies, mail and other paraphernalia. In
addition, she was a floating administrative centre, medical and dental office,
court house, meeting room, purveyor of news and gossip, wedding chapel,
party palace and just about everything else that required a modicum of
civilized accommodation to conduct its affairs. Throw in the navigational
problems and she was a very busy, not to mention vital, servant to everybody
in the North.

To put that vital service into perspective, imagine yourself manning
some small isolated post in the North 75 years before this book came out,
viz. the spring of 1922. There would be one, or possibly two, other HBC
employees there. If you were co-located with a Mountie post or mission,

there would be couple of other whites as neighbors. These would be the only whites within hundreds of kilometres. There would be some natives, both resident and stopping by to trade and visit, and how well you got on with them depended on your linguistic capability. The only means of travel and communication would be by dog sled, canoe, or small open boat. It would involve days of rugged travel to visit the next post and return. You would have no way of communicating with the south. You would have to be totally self-reliant, not only for day-to-day living, but also for dealing with any and all emergencies. You would be living on supplies that you had ordered via Nascopie in the summer of 1920, and had been delivered by her in the summer of 1921. If either you or Nascopie had forgotten any thing back then, you would not be eating it now. Hopefully, it might show up when she returned in three or four months. At that time, you would not only get a year's supplies, but also a year's mail, a year's news and a chance to see some new faces. You would also settle and account for your year's business. If your term was up or you were due for leave, Nascopie was your ride home. Nascopie would sail after a few short days, and the earth would travel all way round the sun before she returned. Obviously, your whole life revolved around shiptime, and if Nascopie didn't make it, the next winter could be even longer and more bitter than the last.

The key passenger, in effect a supernumerary, was the HBC Superintendent for whatever district Nascopie happened to be servicing at the time. Officially, he could route the ship to the various posts in his district and decided what supplies were to be offloaded and returns picked up at each. While Nascopie had what served as radio in those days, the posts did not, so the the only means he had to communicate with them was by visit-

Pond Inlet

ing them in NASCOPIE. At shiptime at each post he was a very busy man, as he had to cover a year's paperwork with the factor in a day or two. This work included the vital listing of supplies to be delivered the next year. (If the lists got back south intact, and the Company accepted them, and the orders were placed with the suppliers, and the suppliers got the stuff delivered to the shed in Montreal, and it was loaded aboard NASCOPIE in the right sequence, and NASCOPIE made it back to the post the next year, the supplies would be delivered. If any link in the chain was broken, they would not.)

On a more esoteric vein, NASCOPIE also carried a postmaster. His job was not only to deliver the mail, but frank it as well. Envelopes with a post mark from an isolated northern post had a certain cachet, not to mention market value, so people from all over would send him mail, complete with a postage paid return envelope. The postmaster would then stamp the latter with the name of the requested post. For many years, Dundas and Craig Harbours, having the highest latitudes, were the favourites. So while NASCOPIE steamed her appointed rounds, the postmaster would be down in his cabin going stamp, stamp, stamp.

Even into the forties and the advent of air service, NASCOPIE retained her role as mail ship. J. Dillon was third mate at the time and his son Jim reports that he never wrote home from the ship for the simple reason that the mail came south in NASCOPIE. His father would have beaten his own letters home.

However, none of these good men had the authority to tell the Captain how to run and navigate his ship. This was not just Company policy, it was and is a fact in Admiralty law. In reality, communications being what they were, the Captain's word was final as soon as NASCOPIE let go her lines in

NASCOPIE's frank

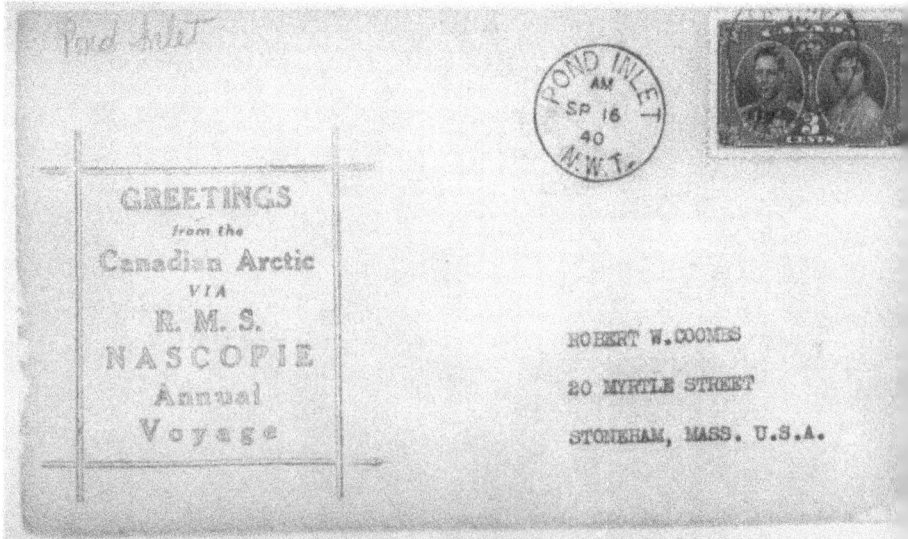

Montreal. If anything happened to the ship, good or bad, he was responsible. That went with the uniform. The Captain seldom stood regular watches, but he was on call twenty-four hours a day, seven days a week. If things started to look dirty up ahead, he took the bridge. He stayed there until he felt things were back on track again, however long that took. In ice, that often meant climbing up into the barrel, exposed to both the elements and the greasy smoke from the funnel, and conning his ship from there, hour after hour.

Running his ship was far from being the end of his duties. In Montreal, he supervised the preparation of a detailed stowage plan to ensure that the cargo was stowed in the correct sequence for unloading at the different posts. He had to mind the ship's stability, because how and where heavy cargo was stowed could affect the ship's rate of roll and steering in a seaway. Deck cargo required particular attention. Heavy seas coming aboard could damage or shift it. Moreover, work had to be done on deck all the time, so the crew had to be able to move about freely. In addition to the cargo and passengers, the ship had to complete its own bunkers and stores. The Captain would not do all this himself, but he was accountable for making sure that it was all done. Finally, on his return to the south, all the back-haul passengers and cargo would have to be offloaded and there were those 14 reports to be completed.

The expression "...and other duties as required" applied to him as well. He was not only Nascopie's Captain, but a relatively senior, and oftentimes only, representative of the Company as well. Whatever problems afloat or ashore that required some kind of Authority to sort out could fall into his lap. Sometimes, simply an extra hand was required and he would pitch in. Captain Smellie, for instance, prided himself on his ability to pour foundations when new buildings were being put up. He would further cement his august position as Captain by passing out the traditional tot that signified completion of construction.

The Reindeer Express

Nascopie opened the twenties in great style by striking a shoal in James Bay on her 1920 voyage, but no serious damage was done. For her 1922 trip, she took on one of her more interesting cargoes. The North was running short of caribou, which were essential for survival by the Inuit. Somebody hit on the idea that they could be replaced by reindeer, which the Inuit could be taught to herd. That somebody also figured there might be other markets for the meat as well. Reindeer herds would be run as they were in Lapland, with the Company turning a profit on the sale of their meat and hides. Reindeer grazed on lichen and Baffin Island had lichen, so there should be no problem, according to the desk hounds in London. Continuing to think big, they then proceeded to place an order for 14,000 head. That spring, Nascopie sailed for Norway, where she loaded 689 reindeer, 3000 bags of moss and some Lap herders to train the Inuit. She delivered her cargo (less 149 deer that didn't survive the trip) to Amadjuak, on the Hudson Strait coast of Baffin Island. She then headed for Lake Harbour to discharge 200 tons of coal, before returning south and then back to Scotland. Unfortunately for the planners, Baffin lichen is not the same as Norwegian lichen, and the reindeer did not take to it. Indeed, many got the hots for the local cariboo, and took to the hills with them. The project was written off.

Captain Smellie then rejoined the ship. A few months before, he had been in command of BAYRUPERT when she struck that rock off the Labrador coast and sank. In most shipping firms, a captain that had just lost its newest vessel would be lucky enough to have a job, much less another command. HBC, however, had been sailing these waters, and risking ships, for over 250 years. They well knew that a captain could not be faulted for hitting a rock that was not where it was supposed to be. Smellie took Nascopie on her first trip north of the Strait, up the Baffin coast and into the High Arctic. While she established a new post at Clyde River, nothing else of note was reported, even though she was probably the deepest draft ship ever to navigate these uncharted waters. After this voyage, she returned to Ardrossan on the Firth of Clyde, which was both her home and wintering port for the next nine years.

Amputation

When Nascopie was anchored at Chesterfield Inlet during her 1924 voyage, a legendary character arrived on board. He was Peter Freuchen, the Danish polar explorer. He had sailed to Thule, Greenland on this, his latest trip in 1921. He had spent the winter of 1923-1924 near Repulse Bay, north of Southampton Island, where his toes had become frozen and then gangrenous. When navigation opened, he had sailed down to Chesterfield to meet Nascopie and have his toes amputated by her doctor. The accounts of this operation, Freuchen's included, differ, but it went something like as follows.

Freuchen was first put under by ether. One of the side-effects of this early anesthetic is that the patient, particularly when going under and coming out, becomes disoriented. He may also get the idea that the world, particularly the people operating on him, are not exactly on his side. He may also choose to tell them so. Peter so chose. Now one of the main advantages of the English language is the great variety and power of its cuss words. No other language can touch it in this respect. In order to express the full scope of his displeasure at the doctor, therefore, Peter quickly switched from inadequate Danish to full-blown English cussin'. This had the further advantage that everyone within a couple of hundred metres could both hear and understand his imprecations. Since the operation was being done at the post rather than aboard Nascopie out in the bay, there was a large audience. It was a sterling performance all round and the operation was successful. It became one of Smellie's many legends.

RESCUE!

In 1925, because NASCOPIE could no longer handle the expanding commitments, the Company put the new ship BAYESKIMO into service, primarily to serve the posts on the Bay. HBC had purchased her "off the ways", i.e., from another owner who was building her. The Company had added some ice strengthening to her conventional hull, but she was certainly no NASCOPIE. In the North, NASCOPIE encountered her off the Button Islands, at the entrance to the Strait. She was beset in the pack with a broken steering gear. It took Smellie six hours to work his ship in to her and rig a tow. He then took her into Port Burwell where repairs were made. After he had seen her fit to sail again, Smellie set off for Lake Harbour while BAYESKIMO made for Fort Chimo. The next day, July 23, while in heavy ice off Lake Harbour, Smellie received an S.O.S. from the other ship at 3.00 p.m. She was seriously beset and sinking in Ungava Bay, over 250 km southeast of his position. Smellie immediately reversed course and headed for the casualty. At 13 knots, this distance could have been covered in about 11 hours, but heavy ice lay between the two vessels and, even with everything the engine room could give him, it took Smellie 16. He was guided by smoke on the horizon and arrived on scene to find the crew and passengers camped on the ice. The morning before BAYESKIMO had been holed by the pressure ice, and

Chief Steward Arthur Reed

her pumps could not hold the water, so they had to abandon ship. To keep themselves warm, they built large fires from blankets and hides soaked in oil. The fires gave off not only heat, but also light and smoke, so they would guide NASCOPIE both night and day. The stranded people had luck from the weather as well. Strong winds could have started their floe working, making it an unsafe platform, and snow could have blinded NASCOPIE. Fortunately, both held off until after NASCOPIE got the people aboard and ferried them back to Port Burwell. From here, they were able to take passage south on another ship while NASCOPIE headed back into the Strait to continue her rounds.

Rescue work is the real test of a ship. When lives are at stake, the ship herself must be put at risk. She has to be driven beyond anything her designers envisaged and be kept at it until the operation has been completed. Damage in rescue work is accepted, and the fact that NASCOPIE came through without any says volumes about her Tyne-side builders.

In 1926, NASCOPIE penetrated even further into the High Arctic, establishing posts at Arctic Bay and on the northeast coast of Somerset Island. However, with the creation of the Arctic Fur Reserve in 1927, which banned trapping in those areas, both posts were closed.

That year, NASCOPIE did not visit the High Arctic, but did two trips into the Bay out of St. John's, one of the few years a double trip was made. In the spring of 1927 also, NASCOPIE went sealing again, as she did for the next two, before heading north for the summer. After her 1930 trip, she returned to her Scottish port. She did not sail from there again until three winters and two summers had passed.

ELEVEN:

THE THIRTIES

Lay-up and Refit

The thirties opened with the world sliding rapidly down the steep slope into depression. As the world slid, so slid fur prices, particularly for white fox, now the Company's mainstay. HBC was obliged to "downsize", a modern euphemism for paring staff, operations and future plans to the bone. NASCOPIE was sent off into what turned out to be a three year lay-up in Scotland, with her duties taken up by the less costly, but much less capable S.S. UNGAVA under charter. However, in the North, things were developing. Churchill was now open, and this port would have a profound effect on the Company's operations. With the port came the grain trade through the Bay and Strait. As the grain ships were thin-skinned conventional hulls, and their crews were unused to these waters, this trade had to be supported. It required communications, aids-to-navigation and icebreaking. Starting in 1927, the government established radio stations at Port Burwell, Wakeham Bay and Nottingham Island. Twelve lighted beacons were placed in the Strait and Bay. Then, in 1930, it launched the N.B. McLEAN, an icebreaker of 6,500 indicated horse power. While NASCOPIE's crew might have felt good about having the most able ship in the North, I suspect they felt even better knowing that there was another ship around capable of reaching them if they needed help. However, as McLEAN's duties were primarily in and about the Strait, NASCOPIE would have to wait a while if she called for assistance when she was in the High Arctic.

When UNGAVA proved incapable of doing the job, it was decided to return NASCOPIE to service. However, she returned in both a different technical configuration and a different concept of operations in order to meet the requirements of new trades.

Technical

There was a growing demand for passenger services in the North beyond the normal transport of Company personnel, missionaries, Mounties and other odds and ends. The government was looking for a cheap way to establish an Arctic patrol and, since NASCOPIE was going just about everywhere that government wanted to go, it seemed logical to simply place a small party of about ten on board. It would tour the Arctic each year and then report back to Ottawa what was happening in that 40% of the country the government was supposed to be running. This party, under the redoubtable Major McKean, was over and above NASCOPIE's normal trade in Mounties. Secondly, there was a growing cruise market. [The Depression was not depressing everybody.] With the opening of Churchill, cruisers could travel from Montreal via the Strait and Bay ports to Churchill. Alternatively, they could board at Churchill, visit the High Arctic and then sail south to Montreal. NASCOPIE was therefore refitted to carry up to 50 passengers in reasonable comfort. Along with expanded accommodation, NASCOPIE also received refrigeration. Now she could not only serve fresh food aboard, but also bring it to any post who could store it, or at least eat it up quickly.

For navigation, NASCOPIE received two invaluable instruments. The first was a gyrocompass, which was much more immune to the wild variations of the North Magnetic Pole than the magnetic compass. The second was a depth sounder. Since the ship spent much of her time in uncharted, barely charted, and/or inaccurately charted waters, this was a real asset.

Other useful equipment included the radios that were being installed in the posts. Now, NASCOPIE could talk to them and they could talk to each other. Of course, nobody yet knew anything about sun spots or other northern phenomena that interfered with transmission, but even poor reception was a big advance over no communication at all.

By this time, it had finally dawned on the powers-that-be that NASCOPIE was spending an awful lot of time swinging around her hook off the posts, waiting for weather suitable for lightering operations. While they could not do anything about the weather, they could take steps to ensure that, when it was good, lightering could proceed as efficiently as possible. Two wooden barges, each powered by twin gasoline engines, were constructed. One was 10.4 m in length and the other 9.4. Each could carry up to 15 tons, depending on the cargo mix. They were based and maintained at Cartwright. One advantage of this was that NASCOPIE would leave Montreal already below her marks. The inspectors, who had already passed her deep draft in Montreal fortunately would not see her after she picked up her barges. These weighed about seven tons each and put her even lower in the water.

The increased passenger complement, new equipment and expanded workload required more people, so her crew was gradually increased to around 50.

While not immediately related to NASCOPIE, aircraft were poking their noses tentatively into the North. Eventually, these would provide year round transportation about the Arctic. Just as important, they could provide ice reconnaissance for vessels, allowing them to know in advance what they would be up against and thus be able to avoid the worst conditions.

Operations

NASCOPIE would no longer be home-ported in Scotland. Her new home was to be Montreal, where she would winter if there was no other work for her. This would avoid having to move crews across the Atlantic every year to pick her up in the spring and deliver her in the fall. Her "returns" would cross to London as cargo in regular vessels. In addition, she would no longer be managed by Head Office in London. Her affairs would be controlled by the Company's main Canadian office in Winnipeg.

Churchill Harbour circa 1931

The opening of Churchill was of vital importance. Now she would not have to sail from Montreal with all the passengers and supplies she was to deliver throughout the North, plus bunker all the coal required to deliver them. She could depart Montreal carrying only the people and material destined for the Strait and part of the Bay. At Churchill, she could pick up more people, supplies and bunkers for the rest of the Bay and the High Arctic. A thousand tons less of coal loaded in Montreal meant a thousand tons more displacement for cargo. (One advantage coal had over oil in the North is that it did not require heated storage and pipelines. Coal could be dumped anywhere, and shifted by wheel barrow, if necessary. Often, it was necessary.) Another commodity she could replenish in Churchill was fresh water. Even if she arrived there with plenty, it had probably been in her tanks at least a month, so new fresh water was welcome. Occasionally, she did draw water from the melt pools on top of the ice if all the salt had been leached out, but this was a slow process. All these new developments did not reduce her workload, however. For instance, in 1936, Nascopie visited 35 ports, from Labrador to the high Arctic.

On June 16, 1933, after a grand send-off by the Governor, Nascopie departed Ardrossan bound Montreal for the last time. She would see the British Isles only once more in her life. Her trip into the North saw her first cruising passengers, six Americans and three Germans. She also carried her first government party, 10 men, plus 23 Company men, women and children, 14 Mounties, 10 missionaries, 5 men from Revillon Freres, a competing fur trade company (a sold berth is a sold berth), an explorer, a King's Scout and a photographer from The Beaver. She also transported a total of 15 Inuit amongst various posts. This passenger list could be considered typical of that era. That voyage took her to Dundas Harbour on Devon Island, Craig Harbour on Ellesmere and then across to Robertson Fiord in Greenland. At lat. 77 deg 40 min. N, this is the farthest north she had sailed to date. Interestingly enough, this fact was not considered particularly noteworthy. Nascopie was expected to do these things.

The Governor's Grand Tour

On the 1934 voyage, Nascopie did herself proud. While the Company had been trading in the North since 1670, no Governor in London had ever seen fit to visit his outposts there, although State visits had been bestowed on the Montreal and Winnipeg offices. Coupled with the fact that he would never see his ship again unless he came out to Canada, Governor P. Ashley-Cooper decided to remedy this oversight. He, Mrs. Ashley-Cooper and his staff, including a piper, Staff Sergeant Hannah, joined the ship in Montreal for the trip north. Each evening, the Sergeant would parade the deck serenading the passengers with doleful Scottish airs, whether they wanted the noise or not. Captain Smellie, whose duties often only permitted him to grab a few hours sleep at odd times, was not amused. The Governor's staff had prepared a detailed itinerary for each stop, totally ignoring the fact that Mother Nature, in the form of ice and weather, controlled NASCOPIE's schedule, not the Governor. Needless to say, the itinerary was soon scrapped.

The first stop was Cartwright.

Len: "I happened to be there when the ship arrived and the Governor presented me with a fine hunting knife with the Company flag and good wishes in syllabic engraved on the blade. Unfortunately, the knife, as well as a rifle that the Fur Trade Commissioner, Ralph Parsons, had given me were both lost when NASCOPIE was wrecked at Cape Dorset."

At Port Burwell, the sergeant, in full regimentals, piped the party ashore. The greeters included just about everybody in the port plus a group of very large huskies. Their opinion of this kilted specimen, emitting weird noises from his instrument, i.e. would he make good eating? was of some interest to the watchers until the dogs had satisfied their curiosity and wandered off. It could have gone either way. True to the traditions of his regiment in battle, Sergeant Hannah "never missed a note", according to the Captain. As for the Inuit, they were enthralled by both his strange garb and stranger music. The good sergeant was the hit of the tour.

The next crisis occurred as they crossed Hudson Bay. Aug. fourth was the 324th anniversary of Henry Hudson's discovery of the Bay, and the plan

Governor Ashley Cooper, Captain Smellie and officers

was to cast a commemorative wreath onto its waters that day. The wreath had been created by the distinguished Royal Empire Society in London and Governor Ashley-Cooper attached considerable importance to the event. He had even prepared a rather impressive speech to mark the occasion. The night before, Captain Smellie ordered his long-standing and long-suffering Chief Steward, Arthur Reed, to fetch the wreath from the refrigerator. The conversation was purported to have gone as follows:

> Reed: "The wreath?"
> Smellie: "The Henry Hudson wreath. Bring it to my cabin."
> Reed: "I never saw a wreath."
> After a panicky search, it was realized that the wreath was still sitting in Montreal.
> Smellie: "Make a wreath. By tomorrow."

The next morning, Good Steward Reed produced a wreath. He had roped in a lady passenger who was a bit of an artist, and the two had spent all night making up a wreath out of wire covered with moss, decorated by flowers made out of toilet paper died with the Captain's red ink. The elaborate ceremony went off flawlessly.

Someone had hit upon the idea that the Governor should address each post the night before the ship reached it and some elaborate broadcasting gear had been installed in the Captain's day room for this purpose. It was to be a sort of warm-up exercise to prepare the minions for the Great Man's coming ashore there the next day. The program included the Governor's address, the pipes and some recorded music. The post about to be honoured would, in theory, be well primed. Unfortunately, the Governor was unaware of the vagaries of radio transmission in the North, and his impressive programs seldom reached their audiences. However, being good Company minions, most were too polite to tell him so.

The Governor learned perhaps more than he really wanted to know about northern travel. His plans kept on getting skewed by ice, weather, missed connections and poor communications. However, both he and Mrs. Ashley-Cooper took it in the right spirit and they certainly understood and appreciated Captain Smellie's professionalism. The Governor boarded his special train in Churchill a man now wise to the ways of the North.

The press across Canada had followed the voyage and made people aware of the vital nature of NASCOPIE's work in the North. Now she could no longer ease quietly out of Montreal Harbour in July and plug her way quietly into northern waters. Now her annual departures were an event. On July 15, 1936, the Montreal Gazette reported in part:

> "That brave little veteran of the Arctic seas, the Royal Mail Ship NASCOPIE is on her long way this morning to the top o' the world.
>
> As she steamed out of Montreal yesterday, ablaze with pennants and her red ensign flying proudly at her stern, and as ships in the harbour spoke with blasting whistles a last farewell, the ice scarred vessel was breaking contact with big cities for three months. Ten thousand

miles of voyaging lay before her, and a mission of trade, of relief and law and order, and of mercy, that stretches to within 800 miles of the Pole.

... It is the story of one of the few adventures left on earth, and Montreal, having seen the Nascopie sail so many times, has nevertheless never tired of the drama and the romance of this little ship as she puts out into the stream.

When she went yesterday morning there were crowds to see her off. On her decks stood red-coated men of the Royal Canadian Mounted Police, going north on the long patrol of law and order that stretches across the eastern Arctic. There were priests and scientists and doctors-each with a mission in the Arctic-and in her holds were loaded the supplies, the medicines and the equipment that mean the difference between life and death to the men who stand guard in the Far North.

... The crowds on the pier waved arms and handkerchiefs and hats in a last too-quick farewell. There were tears in many eyes. Some of those figures on the heavily loaded decks were leaving for long vigils in the Arctic that would last one, three or five years...

She continued on her way, the crowds still lingering on the pier, still waving, and as she steamed downstream the ships in the harbour, all the way to Vickers and below, said good-bye to her with shrill whistles."

Perhaps the "shrill whistles" were the real tribute. The crowds ashore probably only had a general idea of what her voyage would involve, but the mariners knew, and they knew their own vessels could not go where Nascopie was going, nor do what Nascopie would be doing, so they saluted her and wished her good luck and God speed.

Mounties at ease

THE NORTH WEST PASSAGE

For centuries man had been seeking a way to sail a ship from the Atlantic to the Pacific across the top of North America. It proved impossible under sail. The first passage-maker, Roald Amundsen, had used both sail and steam in his little GJOA. However, it had taken the equivalent of three navigation seasons to complete the passage. For the Company, it was not simply a matter of trying an experimental probe that might or might not make it, given unlimited time, but establishing a viable shipping route. The problem was that there were two sectors of very heavy ice at opposite ends of the route; Lancaster Sound north of Baffin Island and Point Barrow at the northern tip of Alaska. With the ships of the day, neither could be passed much before mid August, and the ships had to be clear of them by late September. Unless she was an effective icebreaker, a ship simply could not transit one, sail through the intervening lighter ice, and then clear the other in that time. A complete passage would require two seasons, which was not economical.

The Company thought it might have a better idea. In 1928, the HBC schooner FORT JAMES out of St. John's had sailed into the North and spent two winters at Gjoa Haven on the east coast of King William Island. She was originally to stay only one winter, but the Company was sometimes flexible in these matters. She was tasked to try and find a way to supply the western posts from the east as well as check out the local area for furs. At the end of her stay, the schooner FORT McPHERSON, bringing supplies from the western Arctic had rendezvoused with her there, thus setting a precedent, of sorts. That is the official story, mainly because it coincided with FORT JAMES' original orders. However Len happened to meet with her Chief Engineer who told him the following. During her time in Gjoa Haven, the ship had stopped maintaining her log. This was acceptable because she was technically laid up. In the spring of 1930, she did not want to wait around

The Northwest Passage

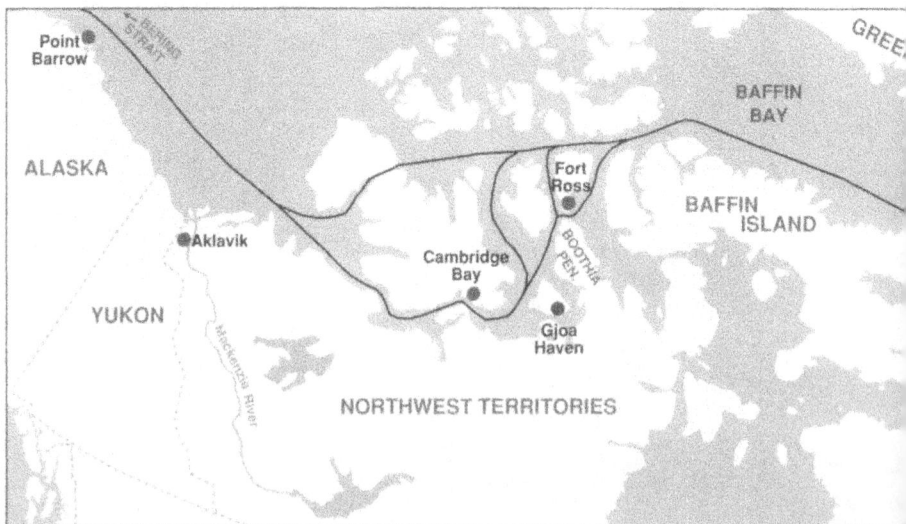

FORT McPHERSON and EL SUEÑO, Cambridge Bay, 1925

for FORT McPHERSON, so she sailed to Cambridge Bay to intercept her. Having taken her stores from McPHERSON, the FORT JAMES headed back, resuming her log opposite Gjoa Haven. She arrived back in St. John's in the fall. In the spring of 1931, she sailed for the west coast via the Panama Canal and thence up into the Western Arctic to Cambridge Bay. In effect, she had completed the North West Passage, albeit in two stages. However, as she had both broken official orders and not kept a log while underway to Cambridge Bay and back to Gjoa to do it, she could never admit to that fact. When deciding which version to accept, bear in mind both that the two places are only about 400 km, or two days' steaming apart and that the crew were a bunch of Newfoundlanders obliged to spend a second year locked into the frozen North who were running short of grub and just wanted to pick up some and get the hell home.

During much of NASCOPIE's lay-up from 1930 to 1933, Captain Smellie had been stationed in Edmonton with the task of improving the Mackenzie River route into the western Arctic. He had brought in new equipment, improved the route and selected a possible site for a harbour on the coast near the mouth of the river. In addition, HBC already had a chain of posts stretching from Aklavik on the river east along to Victoria Strait. However, there was a gap between that strait and their next post east, at Arctic Bay. Finally, in the south, there were railways running across the country. What all this meant was the possibility of a north west passage without Point Barrow. The plan for 1937 was to load a vessel at the mouth of the Mackenzie, transit the easy ice through Coronation Gulf, Queen Maude Gulf and north or south about King William Island to the Boothia Peninsula. This ship would not have to have a heavy icebreaking capability. On the Boothia, she would meet up with NASCOPIE from the east and exchange people and cargo. To complete the scheme, a post would be established on the northern tip of the Boothia which would also tap into the furs in that area. (When they arrived at the site, they were greeted by beautiful white fox, running about the shore. The fox had never seen a ship before and

Landing supplies at Wolstenholme

didn't know what was coming at them.) The post would be called Fort Ross and located on Bellot Strait, a narrow channel separating Somerset Island from the Boothia Peninsula. It was a complex scheme, greatly dependent on the benevolence of Mother Nature, particularly regarding the generally severe ice conditions in Prince Regent Inlet. There was only a brief "window" of the first week in September when NASCOPIE would have her best chance of travelling down Prince Regent Inlet, joining the motor schooner AKLAVIK from the west, erecting the post and getting clear of the Inlet again. There was also the point that no ship had ever transitted Bellot Strait, so even that part was a gamble.

NASCOPIE serviced the Baffin Island posts as she worked north through the summer, having that first week in September always in mind. She then turned west through heavy ice in Lancaster Sound, and then south into Prince Regent Inlet. There were no charts for these waters, so she went by echo sounder and feel. If the icebergs were drifting, the water was deep. If they were aground, it was shallow. No particular site had been chosen for the post and, in one respect, that was good. The man who was going to have to bring the ship in there in future years was right on scene to help with the selection. Captain Smellie would ensure that he had good approaches and a secure anchorage for his ship, and the shore party would pick a site handy to it. (In later years, when weather station and DEW line sites were being selected, the requirements of the supply vessels and landing cargo were not given appropriate consideration, causing all kinds of supply problems for the Coast Guard.) Captain Smellie first cruised the shoreline by boat until he found a bay that met his requirements. The shore party could now select a site on that bay. He then sounded and buoyed a safe approach and brought NASCOPIE in. It was the morning of September one, and there was no sight of AKLAVIK. As this vessel had no radio, they had no idea whether she was on her way or stuck in the ice somewhere to the west. There was no time to waste, so materials for the buildings had started to flow ashore when AKLAVIK's masts were sighted in Bellot Strait and soon she came alongside. After a brief ceremony and a message to Montreal announcing her arrival, it was back to work. Over one side, NASCOPIE was sending materials and supplies ashore, and over the other, exchanging supplies and trade goods for furs from AKLAVIK. In addition, NASCOPIE received her first passenger from the west. Captain Gall of the AKLAVIK was returning home via the North West Passage. Ashore, construction went on almost round the clock. The crews of both ships, as well as the Inuit NASCOPIE had brought along to trap the region, pitched in. A complete post, including store with a section for the Post Office (another sign of Canada's sovereignty), residence and warehouse had to be up and running in seven days. It was, and on the seventh day, Captain Smellie posted a letter to his mother in England from the Fort Ross Post Office. NASCOPIE then hauled anchor and sailed, (presumably carrying the captain's letter) only a day or two ahead of the new ice.

Smellie's signal to Montreal was picked up by both CBC and the BBC and broadcast with the opening, "A 400-year old dream has come true." On her return to Montreal, NASCOPIE was lionized, and Canadian politicians naturally tried to bask in some of the reflected glory. Smellie did not go along with this. As far as he was concerned, HBC was British, he was British, NASCOPIE flew the (British) red ensign and her crew came from (then British) Newfoundland. Canada had had nothing to do with the trip. He was about half right. Canada provided both the land and the furs, which were the whole object of the exercise. If you are going to establish a shipping route, you need something to ship. In fact, other than the establishment of Fort Ross, nothing very practical came out of this expedition. There were easier ways to ship furs out of the western Arctic than trying to make a chancy link-up at Fort Ross.

Northern dentistry

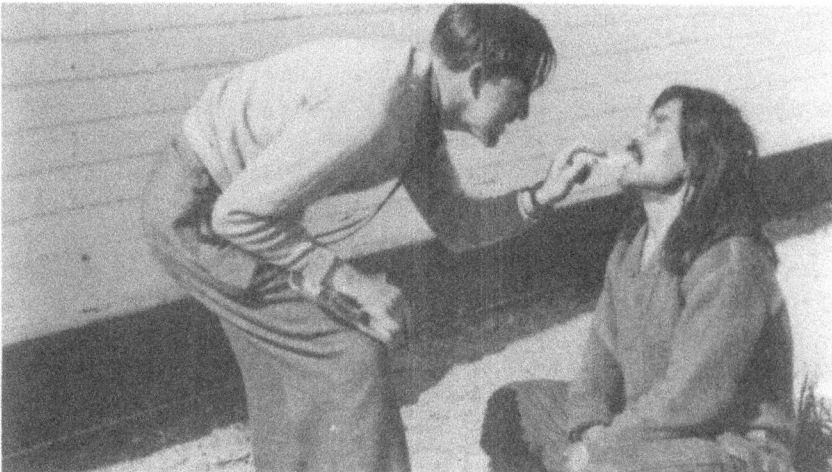

For that matter, Smellie didn't have much use for the Canadian Government's efforts in the North, period. As far as he could see, their only contribution was their people on board his ship. He also thought that the Mounties, with their spit and polish, were not doing much good either. He couldn't understand why they wore spurs aboard, which were damaging the rubber covers on the steps of his companionways. He also did not understand Canada's need to show sovereignty, when she lacked the resources to do it properly. However, the government knew that sovereignty was expressed by presence, and presence was shown by flags and uniforms, even if there were not very many of them. Furthermore, Captain Smellie had never wintered in the Arctic. He had only seen the North from the comfort of his own ship. Months of isolation in lonely posts and long patrols across the barrens in the depths of winter by dog sled, which the Mounties would have to make, were totally beyond his experience. The Mounties he saw had no duties on board and were entitled to relax. They were either headed up to a long posting in the North, or returning from one. However, when the Mounties expressed a desire for their own vessel, he was right in chuckling. Whatever they got, it would be neither as capable nor as comfortable as NASCOPIE. Furthermore, they would have to load and unload their own gear, rather than having a ship's crew do the stevedoring for them. Even when the R.C.M.P. got the famous ST. ROCH, their senior officers preferred to travel in comfort aboard NASCOPIE.

For the rest of her career, Fort Ross was to be the burning issue every year. While NASCOPIE could be flexible everywhere else, it was September one or nothing for Fort Ross. Even then, there was always some doubt. At that small post, the question was "Can she get in?" At the posts she would visit after Fort Ross, the question was "Can she get out?"

NASCOPIE did more than just chauffeur the Governor around and open the North West Passage during the thirties. She humped her stores and passengers, picked up her furs, served as a floating administrative centre for various activities, including hearing two criminal cases, and served as sort of love boat. She delivered brides to bridegrooms, held weddings and christenings on board and carried honeymooners as passengers. My father even considered her for their honeymoon, but they couldn't change their wedding commitments, and the heartless HBC wouldn't alter NASCOPIE's sailing date to accommodate them. (Fort Ross again?)

After the 1938 voyage, NASCOPIE wintered in Halifax. In the spring she sailed across to Falmouth for an extensive refit, her last visit to Britain. She then returned to Montreal, and loaded for the North. Arctic cruising had by then had become so popular that she sailed with 21 tourists. A special Arctic Circle crossing ceremony was held, complete with King Boreas and Queen Aurora. Such festivities would not be held aboard again for six long years. In the summer of 1939, she departed Montreal for the North with the world at peace. She returned in the fall to a world at war.

Twelve:

Again to War

On the way south in that September of 1939, Nascopie was aware that she was once more a belligerent and possible target for submarines. A black-out was instituted and her life boats provisioned and swung out. Before heading north, Captain Smellie had scrounged some grey paint from somewhere, and at every spare moment, the crew had swung down into boats and stages and slapped it on her hull. She proceeded to Halifax where she received her first armament, an ancient machine gun, a couple of rifles and five troops to man them. Guns mounted on merchant vessels in the early part of a war had one thing in common. They were dug out of some forgotten store or even a museum and were so old that they usually scared the people who might have to fire them much more than they scared the enemy. One can only presume that the German fleet did not lose much sleep over this latest addition to allied forces.

In the spring of 1940, Nascopie sailed for Ivigtut on the west coast of Greenland to deliver supplies and load cryolite, an ore for aluminum, from the mine there. At Ivigtut, Nascopie once more ran afoul of war-time bureaucracy and security. Cryolite was considered a strategic material and somebody had forgotten to tell the Danes she was coming. Nascopie was left to swing around her hook for four weeks while the powers-that-be sorted it out. She dropped her cargo at the aluminum refinery at Port Alfred, Que. and proceeded up to Montreal to prepare for the North.

On the voyage into the North, Nascopie delivered an iron lung to the small Church of England run hospital at Pangnirtung, the most northerly medical establishment in the world. Even up there, one could not escape the dreaded polio. On a lighter note, the ship also continued her role as Cupid, as two weddings took place on board.

The 1941 voyage was marked by heavy ice, but Nascopie managed to complete her program, including loading cryolite in Greenland. By now, Captain Smellie was running into a problem that plagued all shipping in war, shortage of good men. During the Depression, shipping had been hit hard. Experienced officers and prime seamen were suffering on the beach, begging for work. Any vessel still sailing could have its pick of them, and for garbage wages. Now, with navies expanding as fast as they could build, and merchant vessels being brought out of Depression lay-up, experienced men were at a premium. Any officer who had served at sea could join the Navy and be almost guaranteed a command. Deck hands would be given stripes right away. (The smart ones knew from World War One that the Germans would target the vessels carrying war supplies, not the escorts, so it would be safer in the Navy. They were right.) Those with mechanical expertise, such as engine room crews, could easily find well-paying work in the expanding factories and mills ashore, far from German submarines. It soon became obvious that not everybody wanted to be a hero. Finally, of course, there were the losses to German subs. Governments tried to hide their extent from the public, but they couldn't hide them from the men who went to sea and shared the same watering holes ashore. Allied seamen were placed in the Manning Pool, and ships' crews were made up from whatever men were available from it at the time. NASCOPIE had to take the men assigned to her, whatever their qualifications. Like all merchant vessels, NASCOPIE was plagued with desertions, which often happened just as she was about to sail.

NASCOPIE under arms. Note life rafts

Fortunately this was never a problem in the North. Who is going to jump ship in a place like Pond Inlet? In the engine room, lack of expertise was a particular problem, because it took years to learn how to get the best out of a coal-fired plant. If a man didn't know how to build and a bank a fire, when to empty ashes and how to control the boiler feed water, he was not going to get all the power the plant could deliver, and her ice capability dropped accordingly. Moreover, the engine room crew were responsible for maintaining all the mechanical and electrical equipment on board, and many were not up to it. Nascopie suffered several equipment problems during the war, usually due to lack of competence in the engine room crew. Fortunately, none of the failures were fatal.

For government, which controlled shipping, the question of what to do with Nascopie was becoming critical. As the war progressed, the North was gaining strategic value. It was no longer just a question of the Company's fur trade and supporting a few Mounties and missionaries. There were ships that could transport people and supplies but couldn't break ice, and ships that could break ice but couldn't transport people and supplies. Only Nascopie could do both so Canada could ill afford to lose her. However, there was also a desperate shortage of shipping. She would, therefore, continue to go north in summer and only undertake voyages on the western side of the Atlantic for the rest of the year. During the winters of 1941 and '42, she tramped from Newfoundland down to the Caribbean, going wherever she was sent and picking up whatever cargo she was sent for. She sailed in convoy to Newfoundland to deliver materials to the new bases the Americans were building, but sometimes her engine room performance was so bad she couldn't even make convoy speed and had to plug along on her own. Once she arrived off St. John's, then a naval base, after the entrance had been closed, and was obliged to steam around outside, where submarines were a possibility, until the port re-opened in the morning. At Charleston, N.C., she was loaded with fertilizer. This is normally shipped in bags, but the stuff was poured directly into her holds, covering her decks with the white powder which contained 20% sulphuric acid. This chemical burned the eyes and it took months to clean the last of it out of the ship. She was being handled by agents in New York, and to them, she was just another freighter to find work for in the western Atlantic.

The 1942 voyage north was a different story. She made, or tried to make, her usual rounds plus a stop for cryolite and spent 135 days between departing Montreal and offloading at Port Alfred, the longest northern voyage of her career. Things advanced smoothly until she turned south into Prince Regent Inlet toward Fort Ross. Nascopie encountered the heaviest ice ever seen there, a mixture of old and new ice and icebergs. The ship gave of her best, although the Captain had some doubts whether the engine was developing its full power, but the ice defeated her. Nascopie was being worked so hard that she was taking damage. Captain Smellie knew how important shiptime was to a post, in terms of both logistics and morale, and it went against his grain to fail to make one. Furthermore, he was operating under mandatory radio silence, so he had no communications. (The posts were not, on the theory that the Axis already knew where they were.) However, Nascopie could not progress. New ice was forming and she had burnt a lot of coal, so 240 km short of Fort Ross, she had to give up trying to reach it. Now she had to concentrate on getting out of the Inlet while she could. The three people in the post were in no danger, however. They still had a year's staples left and, if necessary, additional supplies could be brought in by dog team from Arctic Bay or even air-dropped in from the south. Unfortunately, the people themselves, who were due for transfer, could not get out.

On her way south, along with playing Cupid for a couple of marriages again, she put into Ivigtuk for cryolite, but the mine, as usual, was not ready for her. She was sent off over 25 km to an anchorage where she sat for ten days while running down her bunkers and food stocks. She went down the coast to Julianehaab to coal, but the only coaling facilities there were a couple of women and a skiff. However, the women were willing, so they somehow got 60 tons aboard (Smellie had asked for 200), plus a couple of sheep carcasses for the larder. The social graces were not forgotten, however. They were there on October 11, the 25th anniversary of Captain Smellie first joining Nascopie, and that merited a dinner complete with various toasts. He had joined during one war and was back into it 25 years later. While returning to the mine, they ran into hurricane force winds gusting to 160 k.p.h., forcing Nascopie to head out to sea to avoid being blown ashore. Since she was light, Nascopie rolled like the proverbial drunken sailor, making life rather uncomfortable aboard. Then she stowed her cargo of cryolite, kissed Greenland good-bye and sailed for Port Alfred and home. She never visited Greenland again.

To fill out her crew, the Company would take on university students as their summer vacation time fitted in neatly with Nascopie's northern trip. Students, of course, are generally long on theory and short on practical skills. (I speak from experience.) However, it was decided that they couldn't put the ship at hazard very much if they were assigned to the steward. They had many adventures, but one during the 1942 trip should sum them up. The student/steward T. Coffin wrote it up for the June 1943 Beaver.

> During heavy weather, Captain Smellie was on the bridge and young Coffin went up to take his order.
>
> "The 'Old Man' decided to have soup. 'In a big mug, Steward.' When I took the order back to the pantry, Mr. Reed set the mug on a plate, the whole on a napkin, and brought the corners together at the top.
>
> 'Now,' he said, 'hold it there, and let it swing as free as it likes; it'll never spill."
>
> Of course this was true, but sometimes it was hard to look at that plate and make yourself believe that it was horizontal. Arrived at the bridge, I opened the napkin fold by fold, to make it dramatic, only to have the show spoiled when the curtain went up.
>
> 'Why Steward, how do you expect me to eat this without a spoon?'

Carrying the soup

Poor young Coffin, feeling suitably hard done by, went back down for a spoon. Stuffed full of theory as he was, it never dawned on him to bring a spoon in the first place. Captains and pilots tend to go a little grey on top when they have students aboard. Fortunately, a few of them remember that they were once students themselves.

Strategic considerations were now overtaking furs as the prime activity in the North. New aircraft were being flown to both Britain and Russia, and these air lifts required both refuelling stations en route and reliable weather forecasts. The air route to Britain was across Labrador and/or the North-Greenland-Iceland-Scotland, so air fields were being built at Goose Bay, Churchill, Southampton Island, Fort Chimo and Frobisher Bay (now Iqaluit). Much of the weather affecting these flights originated in the High Arctic, but reporting from the few posts up there was at best, spasmodic. Furthermore, they could only report surface weather. Reporting high altitude conditions required special equipment and balloons to take it up. In 1942, some very hush-hush weather stations, particularly at Arctic Bay, were established by the Americans, which Canada took over the next year. Of course the people and gear had to be taken up there and resupplied and since NASCOPIE was dropping by there anyways, would she mind...? (The secrecy was largely wasted. During the war, a German sub eased into the Labrador coast and erected an unmanned weather station. The thing sat there for over forty years until somebody tripped over it and called the Canadian government.)

Actually, the military was quick to learn that just about anywhere they wanted to go in the North, NASCOPIE regularly visited, along with many places they had never heard of. For the rest of the war, she usually sailed with a few military types aboard. Unfortunately, when the military, especially the U.S. military, take over something, the rest of us are expected to stand aside and be grateful for their presence. Churchill, for instance, was turned into a major military base for Arctic operations. Before the war, NASCOPIE's arrival was an important event there. Now she was relegated to the far end of the wharf, where a small area had been set aside for her to handle passengers and cargo and take bunker. As far as the military was concerned, this ancient coal burner was interfering with their saving the world. Canada took a slightly more sanguine view. The government often did not know exactly what the Americans were doing in its North, and for much of the time, the party aboard NASCOPIE was the only eyes it had up there.

NASCOPIE was not sent tramping in the winter of 1942/43. She wintered in Montreal and prepared for the 1943 trip north. Again, the critical issue was Fort Ross. In 1941, the post had been stocked for the usual outfit year plus one, which meant that her supplies would last until shiptime 1943. If she could not be resupplied then, her people would have no food. NASCOPIE set off on her northern rounds, but was delayed in reaching Prince Regent Inlet until mid-September. At first, passage down the Inlet was easy, but only because northerly winds had pushed the ice to the south. By nightfall, NASCOPIE had reached it and been brought to a halt. They were still over 60 km from the post. The next day, they gained but 50 m. The temperature was below freezing, and ice was forming in the open leads. The following day, a few leads opened up and they were able to steam several km before the ice closed in again. They could just see the entrance to Bellot Strait to the south and were sure the people at Fort Ross could see their smoke as the battle continued. Mr. J.L. Robinson described it in the March, 1944 Beaver.

> "For an hour the ship plunged into the ice. Fourteen times we reversed and came grinding, crashing, pushing forward. Sometimes we made ten yards, but usually less. The youthful enthusiasts on the bow maintained a lively football account of our progress. But at the end of fourteen "bucks into the line" we had made only about two hundred yards and the "touchdown line" was still far away. The tough NASCOPIE seemed to be taking the pounding without damage. She was losing paint from her hull as the ice blocks scraped under her, but otherwise she was plunging ahead like an all-American fullback.
>
> ... It was apparent that it was a hopeless task and a waste of coal to smash through when a storm or a strong wind would break up the pack and give us a lead. Thus, strangely enough, amid the icy emptiness of the bleak Arctic, where storms were the fear of all navigators, about sixty men and two women prayed for a storm."

Since they couldn't move, some of them did the next best thing. They went out on the ice and played baseball. The ice flow they were locked into was carrying them south and they could see new ice forming to the north, the way out of the Inlet, and actually freezing the ship in. They had entered the heavy ice September 16, some 60 km north of Fort Ross. By September 21, they were still 21 km from it, but that was 21 km too far. Fort Ross couldn't be reached and even getting out was looking dicey. The next day they headed north and managed to break their way clear. The mark of a good captain on an important mission is to recognize that point in the operation where the risks to the people and vessel under his command are of greater importance than reaching his objective. There were but three people in the post and other options were available to rescue them. There were 62 on board his ship and his first obligation after reaching that point had to be to them.

Naturally, Mr. and Mrs. Heslop and D. Munroe, the "strandees" at Fort Ross had a different point of view. Barbara Heslop wrote it up for the March, 1944 Beaver.

> "One evening in September, we sighted the NASCOPIE about fifteen miles offshore. We thought our worries were over; but it was not until later that we were to realize that they were just beginning. For three days we saw her, or her smoke, on the horizon and it was evident she was having difficulty in the ice-pack. That was an anxious three days, but we didn't give up until we finally saw her heading north with black smoke belching from her funnel. This called for a conference, and after taking stock of our dwindling supplies we recognized our position was definitely not good. Our foodstuffs were low, and our meals had little variation. For some time we had been without butter, milk, coffee, fruits, and canned vegetables excepting beans. We all became very diligent hunters, always hoping to bag any wild game. Seals as a rule are plentiful at Fort Ross, but owing to the heavy ice-pack we were not able to get as many as we ordinarily would use. Seal livers are very delicious, but seal meat we found too strong for our tastes. Occasionally our day's tramp would be rewarded with an Arctic hare-a real treat."

Baseball on the ice

Obviously, the three were in for a long, hungry winter if something wasn't done, so plans were put in place. While Nascopie had nothing to do with the rescue of the people at Fort Ross, it is still a story worth telling. They were not the only ones running out of food, the local Inuit were on short rations as well. They too had become dependent on Nascopie for at least part of their supplies. That is why they trapped furs. Therefore, the situation was that both whites and Inuit needed food and the whites had to be brought out as well. The Company contacted the Canadian government but Canada had no planes available with sufficient range to do the return flight from the south. Canada therefore approached the U.S. who agreed to help with a C-47 (military version of DC-3), specially fitted with skis over wheels. Extra fuel tanks were installed. Since neither ice nor weather conditions would be suitable until early November, time was taken for careful planning. The first flight consisted of a drop by parachute of several hundred pounds of food, a radio and Captain J. Fletcher of the U.S. Army Air Force, an Arctic specialist. Captain Fletcher had received one whole hour's parachute training but had never actually jumped. I suppose this made him as qualified as any for the first ever parachute jump into the Arctic. On the November one flight, the weather closed in and they had to abort. On November four, both Captain Fletcher and the supplies jumped successfully. His job was to a select a site where the heavy aircraft could land safely. He did not think the sea ice was strong enough yet to bear the plane so he selected a small lake about 16 km from the post, where they proceeded to rough out a runway.

When everything was ready, they called in the aircraft. It managed to get in and when it had taxied up, some of the crew jumped out and swung the tail around. They dare not let the aircraft stop for fear that it would sink in. Additional supplies for the Inuit were dumped out and the passengers boarded on the run. Then the plane lumbered down the runway and eased

Rescue aircraft makes it in

Safe aboard

into the air, clearing the low hills at the end by about three m. It was a near thing, but it showed that aircraft could do a lot more than many thought they could in the North.

Compared to the previous years, 1944 was almost a quiet summer cruise, although NASCOPIE did have to work through some heavy ice in Hudson Strait and northern Hudson Bay. On this trip she made such good time that she slid down Prince Regent Inlet and was anchored off Fort Ross on September one. Three days later, the HBC jack had been raised, the post was back in business and NASCOPIE cleared the anchorage. War may be hell, but love is still love, so NASCOPIE took part in three weddings on this trip. Even more important was her medical function. On this voyage, NASCOPIE carried both a doctor and a dentist to look over the medical and dental problems of the people of the North, both white and Inuit. Canada was recognizing that, while the war brought a lot of new people into the North, it brought a few new medical problems for the residents as well. Being a floating clinic was just one more job for the versatile NASCOPIE to add to her laurels. Since a ship is a totally self-contained and self-supporting community, it has all the inherent requirements to practise medicine in isolated areas.

The 1944 voyage proceeded so smoothly that NASCOPIE had her lines fast in Montreal on October one. The voyage could be considered routine, but is was only routine for a ship called NASCOPIE. It had its share of ice, icebergs, fog, heavy weather,uncharted waters and working cargo into small landing craft and onto rough beaches in marginal conditions. For almost any other vessel in the world, it would have been dangerous if they were lucky, disastrous if they were not. Most likely, they would have passed it off as being impossible. For NASCOPIE, the impossible was routine.

In 1939, NASCOPIE had left the wharf at Montreal in a world at peace and returned to a world at war. In 1945, she sailed in a world still half at war and returned to a world at peace. This voyage was to be historic for a number of reasons. For Captain Smellie and Chief Steward Reed, it was to be their last. Both were heading into retirement after many years of some of the hardest sea-going service in the world. For both, this voyage became a long round of farewells. NASCOPIE also expanded her duties as a mobile clinic. She not only carried two doctors and a dentist, but an oculist, an optometrist and a technician as well. Three eye operations were performed while the ship was underway. It was another relatively easy year for ice, and with the war threat gone, a relaxing trip, but ceremonial as well. At Lake Harbour, "Eskimo Tommie" was presented with the Royal Humane Society Medal for a rescue in 1943. There was a christening at Churchill and a wedding at Pond Inlet. Off Beechey Island in Lancaster Sound a ceremony was held commemorating Franklin's last voyage of 1845-6. At Dundas Harbour, then the most northerly settlement in Canada, the R.C.M.P. reopened its post and post office, with appropriate flourishes. NASCOPIE was present at two trials of Inuit, one at Chesterfield Inlet and the other at Fort Ross. The second might be of interest to certain bread winners who aren't bringing home sufficient bread. A woman had married a man who turned out to be a poor hunter, so she bumped him off. In the North, this is considered just short of justifiable homicide, so she was given what might be considered a suspended sentence.

NASCOPIE arrived back in Montreal on September 26. Captain Smellie was given the salute he earned after so many long tough voyages into the North. He retired, not to Britain, but to Victoria B.C., where he would get the best of both worlds. In 1947, both he and his resolute NASCOPIE died.

Departing Churchill 1945

Thirteen:
Farewell Nascopie

IN 1946, THE WORLD WAS AT PEACE, sort of. The Red Menace was returning to centre stage after being interrupted by the war. Ever since the
Russian Revolution, certain classes on both sides of the Atlantic had
always feared Godless Communism more than the Axis, who at least could
keep the masses docile and make the trains run on time. Stalin was stirring
things up in eastern Europe, Mao Tse Tung was on the march in China, and
the Berlin airlift was only two years down the road. This was no time to let
down the guard. As any Russian attack on North America by air would
come in across the Arctic, that area was being given special attention, particularly by the U.S. If the U.S. was going to do things in Canada's Arctic,
Canada had better be up there itself, or it might find that it had lost much
of its North by default. Officially Canada might own the lands, but if the
U.S. established a bunch of secure facilities up there, Canada might find
itself having to ask U.S. permission to visit a good part of its own territory.
In short, Canada essentially had to raise its own profile in the North by
demonstrating both presence and activity. Of course, Canadians too were
aware of the Red Menace, as well as the fact that Canada couldn't protect
itself on its own, so it had to cooperate. Even the little weather station in
Arctic Bay did its bit for the defense of North America. When one of the
crew decided to mark out the station's call sign on a hill behind the post,
he was deterred by the rest because the Russians might spot it. The fact that
the station sent out weather reports twice a day in clear over the radio, iden-
tifying itself by its call sign, which the Russians could easily track, never
seemed to have come up. One thing that did come up was a U.S. icebreaker,
which refused to tell these Canadian Government employees working in a
"secret" weather station just what it was doing up there. Perhaps there were
two menaces facing Canada in the North. Canada definitely had to be up
there and could no longer rely just on the good offices of the HBC to get its
people around.

Canada was also recognizing her responsibility for the Inuit which she had more or less treated with benign neglect over the years, and this required that she actually put some people in the North to provide some assistance. Better late than never.

Modern armed forces require all kinds of gear to go to war, from bulldozers to battleships to bombers. When the war is over, they simply remove the guns from much of the equipment and declare it surplus. The war effort in the North had left a lot of infrastructure there - air fields, buildings, communications, aids-to-navigation, docks and equipment, much of which was made available to civil authorities and commercial interests. Furthermore the war had stimulated technological development, particularly in the fields of aircraft, communications and electronic navigation. Thus, there was not only a lot of surplus material available, but highly advanced as well. Along with the equipment, there were also plenty of people trained to operate it, particularly pilots, communicators and electronic navigators. In the years immediately after the war, therefore, the North had a strategic significance, a requirement to help the people, an infrastructure and a lot of useful equipment complete with trained operators. In particular, the establishment of air fields and development of rugged bush planes with both floats and skis meant that an "isolated" post was a thing of the past. Even before the war, the Company had operated a small fleet of light aircraft. However, when war broke out, its pilots joined up and HBC donated its planes to the R.C.A.F. as trainers. After the war, the Company picked up a small mixed fleet of aircraft.

Not everything was now all beer and skittles for HBC personnel, though.

Northern landing

R.C.M.P. vessel, St. Roch

Len: "In December 1945, they purchased a Norseman Five for an emergency trip to Repulse Bay. I went north with Harry Winny to relieve the Manager and was there until August 1946. There was absolutely no fuel and no food left in the store. I lived in an unheated house from January until August and hunted for what I ate. I won't say I enjoyed that winter, but it was less boring than operating radio for the Army."

Is that what the Army means with its slogan "There's no life like it"?

One thing that was still in short supply was passenger and cargo carrying icebreakers. So while the bulk of the two militaries packed up their flags and paraded off to cosy billets or demobbing in the south, old coal burning Nascopie, who had been sailing these waters since before many of them were even born, carried on. Even the legendary R.C.M.P. vessel St. Roch under the stalwart Henry Larson could not substitute. As old Arctic hands pointed out, while she was to be admired for her perseverance and fortitude in making the return passage from Vancouver to Halifax, it had taken her four years to do it. All she had really done is navigate, and you don't send ships into the North just to steam around. You send them up there to do something. Actually, she did a little more than just steam around, according to Len. The story was that, one of the reasons she took so long is that her crew were augmenting their per diems by stopping along the way to do a little hunting and trapping. They also point out that she was never more than 200 km from an HBC post, an easy run for a good dog team, so she wasn't exactly alone in the Arctic. This was probably a good thing because St. Roch was never built to work heavy ice. Regardless of her condition when she left Vancouver, she was pretty clapped out when Len, aboard NASCOPIE, met up with her in Pond Inlet. Both her pumps were running full out to keep her afloat, and Captain Smellie donated a 10 cm pump as further insurance to get her to Halifax. For the Arctic hands, their feelings towards the little ship were not professional jealousy. Captain Smellie, for one, was sure that, given reasonable ice conditions, NASCOPIE could have done the Passage in one season, and worked cargo along the way. After all, she routinely did the hardest stretch, Lancaster Sound and Prince Regent Inlet. Once through Bellot Strait, or north about Somerset Island, she would have an easy run to Point Barrow, which is usually passable to the end of September. She could then return east through the Panama Canal. It could have been done, but there was simply no commercial reason for doing it, and glorious headlines don't boost the bottom line.

For 1946, NASCOPIE shed both her war paint and weapons, neither of which had ever proved useful, and fitted radar, which most definitely would. Now she would be able to sight the icebergs, ships and shorelines day or night in any weather, and in plenty of time to take avoiding action. It wouldn't help her in the ice though, it was not sensitive enough to pick out flat surfaces from the water they were floating in. The old mark one eyeball up in the barrel would still be required to find the leads and easiest ice.

She departed Montreal July six under Captain James Waters, who had been her First Officer since 1941. The usual large crowd of potentates and well-wishers were on the wharf to see her off. On board was a large medical complement, an indication of the governments growing concern for the health of the Inuit. Besides the doctors, dentist and oculists, she also carried a team of X-ray technicians. At each port, she would hold full clinics, where the Inuit would be examined and X-rayed to provide a data bank for future activity. NASCOPIE stopped at Cartwright to pick up her two barges and proceeded north, encountering her first ice about 160 km south of Cape Chidley, and having to work it until she cleared Port Harrison (now Inukjuak), on the east side of Hudson Bay.

As stated before, playing Cupid was always one of NASCOPIE's more pleasant duties and on this trip, she was carrying two prospective brides, Wanda Tolboom and Dedie Keighly, to Cape Harrison to join their respective grooms, Wulf and Sam. Presumably, they had last names, but Wanda must have forgotten them. In addition, a prospective groom, "Slim" Harrison, joined the ship at Southhampton Island. He was being transferred to Arctic Bay. His bride was to meet the ship in Churchill where they would be married before leaving for the High Arctic. This plan assumed that his bride would get to Churchill in time to meet the ship. They didn't seem to have a Plan B for if she didn't. Nobody ever said courting in the North was simple. Wanda wrote up the story for the Autumn 1956 Beaver. Her tale opens at Wolstenholme, and the schedule was Cape Dorset-Coral Harbour on Southampton Island-Cape Smith (now Akulivik)-Port Harrison.

Some extracts:

> *Cape Dorset* - "Peering ashore we saw two animated figures tumble out
> of the mission dwelling. Their black robes fluttered in the wind. A
> moment later the mission standard was run to the top of the flagpole and
> the figures went tumbling in again."

That was an appropriate comment on the clergy by a young woman sailing
to her nuptials.

> *At the Coral Harbour meteorological and radio station* - "The long low
> buildings seemed quite deserted. In a gaily adventurous mood we
> skipped down the empty corridors to suddenly confront an extremely
> astonished group of men lounging in a dormitory.
>   'Good God! Women!' shouted one."
>
> "But even he was too paralyzed to move. Not only were they
> unaware that a NASCOPIE party had come ashore, but the poor fellows
> had only seen one white woman in a year or more. And there we stood
> in the doorway gaping like a couple of goons. We never missed a thing
> and the poor unfortunate boys knew it. Toes protruded from mismated
> socks. Shaves and haircuts were notable by their absence. From the walls
> and even the ceilings hundreds of pin-up girls gave us round-eyed stares.
> Never have I seen so many reproductions of undraped female flesh all
> in one room."

That evening they returned and did what most people in the Arctic do
when new people arrive, they partied.

Wanda's trousseau

In heavy ice on the way to Cape Smith - "I forget what Dedie did. I was occupied with quietly going crazy at the delay. When I put my parka on and stuck my nose out of doors, the ship would be zigging. When I repeated the procedure, she would be zagging. Finally, I gave up and decided to use my pent up energy in laundering some clothes. So I monopolized the ladies bathroom (which was also the laundry) for an entire afternoon. At last I completed the job and the irate line-ups outside the door finally got moving. But no one seemed to appreciate the preview of 'what the bride wore' that hung limp and dripping from every hook, line and steam pipe in the room."

The voyage from Cape Smith to Port Harrison, which normally took about 26 hours, required seven days, such was the ice.

"The ship no longer searched for passage-ways around the ice. Instead she looked for crevices into which she might point her bow and ram her way ahead. We were now travelling against the ice [which was drifting northward towards the Strait] and it milled and crashed around us with tremendous force."

When she heard they might not be able to make Port Harrison, Wanda

"went wailing to Mr. Anderson [District Manager]. Highly distraught, I blurted out: 'Oh whatever shall I do if we can't get in?'

'Why,' he replied smilingly, 'nothing at all. You will get off at Churchill, go home by rail and try again next year.'

It was as simple as all that! What an appalling thought! I went down to my cabin, crawled into my bunk and pulled the covers over my head."

Captain Walters must have assumed that, if Nascopie didn't make it, he was going to wind up with two screaming meemies on his hands, so he pressed on and made Port Harrison, where the much delayed nuptials proceeded as planned. We are not advised whether Slim had the same luck in Churchill.

After the heart-throbbing tension at Port Harrison, the rest of the voyage could only be anticlimactic. It was good to see the grain ships sailing from Churchill for hungry Europe once again. Heading up the Baffin Coast and into the High Arctic, Nascopie had only easy ice to contend with. While Fort Ross was reached with no problem, Captain Walters only tarried there 14 hours. There were other stops to be made. That voyage saw Nascopie visit 20 ports and steam over 16,000 km. She arrived back in Montreal October three, after completing what was to be her final round trip voyage into the North.

NASCOPIE'S LAST VOYAGE

On a hot, sunny July five, 1947, Royal Mail Ship Nascopie, all flags flying, cast off her lines from the wharf in Montreal. On the dock, dozens stood waving good-bye. Besides her crew of 50, she carried 32 passengers, all of whom had duties to perform in the North. There were the Company servants, medical people, Mounties, missionaries and other types who were travelling north for a variety of reasons. Once more she put into Cartwright to take aboard her barges. The ice was easy all the way up into Hudson Strait. In the Strait, she stopped in at Lake Harbour, Sugluk and Wolstenholme. Then, on the morning of July 21, she departed that post and headed across the Strait to Cape Dorset. The sky was cloudy but the sea was smooth and almost free of ice. At the approaches to Cape Dorset, Captain Waters decided to enter without the pilot. Suddenly, her depth sounder warned of rocks close ahead and not shown on the chart. Moreover, their slopes were nearly vertical, so she had almost no warning. Although she threw her engine full astern, she struck, and struck hard. At first, she would not come off, but as the tide rose, and with her engine full astern, she floated free and the anchor was let go. However, she was badly damaged, the pumps could not keep up with the incoming water, and that night, the weather began to deteriorate. About 3.00 a.m., the anchor was raised and she attempted to get underway again. However, with the water in her and no way on for steerage, she was unmanageable in the current and she struck

NASCOPIE aground

Farewell NASCOPIE

again. Again her engine was put full astern, but her stern swung into another part of the reef and she was finished. Fortunately, she was so hard aground that there was no danger of her going down immediately, so an S.O.S. went out and all her people were taken ashore in boats from both the ship and the Cape Dorset post, where they crowded into the tiny settlement. Over the next two days, they managed to salvage from her all the mail, some of the food, the ship's bell and a few other souvenirs. I find their priorities interesting. They salvaged the bell but didn't try to save any of her expensive electronic equipment. On the 23rd, the Company's Canso flew in from Churchill with more food and took out 11 Company passengers, leaving the crew and everybody else. None of this old fashioned "women and children first" stuff, and the aircraft did not return. As soon as the government had received NASCOPIE's signal, it had ordered the N.B. McLEAN to steam up from the Strait of Belle Isle to recover the remaining passengers and crew. The ship took them and, presumably, the bell aboard and sailed for Churchill to land them for the train south.

NASCOPIE remained on her lonely rock until October 15, when she finally slid off and sank in deep water nearby. In some respects it was not a sad ending. She was due to be taken out of service in a year or two anyways, and would probably have ended her days as a coal hulk or garbage scow in some nameless backwater. It might have been a little more fitting if she had reached the High Arctic, where she had fought her toughest battles, before being lost. However, she started her career in the North by sailing into Hudson Strait, so the Strait was a noble enough place to end it.

POSTSCRIPT:

AFTER NASCOPIE

THE COMPANY NEVER REPLACED NASCOPIE with another passenger and cargo carrying icebreaker. The market for furs had seriously fallen off and most of HBC's energies in Canada were being put towards its expanding retail trade in the south. The Company now ran a growing chain of department stores across Canada. Furthermore, as the Inuit were now receiving social welfare, many of her stores in the North were now selling goods to the Inuit for cash, rather than furs. Finally, the government was developing its own marine transportation system for the North. For the

The new way. Chopper aboard C.D. HOWE

interim, therefore, HBC could meet its limited needs by charter. NASCOPIE'S replacement was a rather modest vessel in comparison. Launched in Scotland in 1949, RUPERTLAND was only 55.7 m in length and 660 tons, compared to NASCOPIE's 93.6 m and 2520.2 tons. While she was steel hulled and diesel powered, she could never hope to emulate NASCOPIE in the ice, and never tried. The farthest north she ever reached was Pangnirtung on the Baffin coast.

A good part of NASCOPIE's activity had been government work. However, in 1945, the government had decided to build its own vessel, and design work had begun for what was to be the C.D. HOWE. At her keel laying at the Davie Shipyard in Lauzon, Que., February 18, 1948, the Hon. Lionel Chevrier, Minister of Transport, stated:

> "For many years past Government officials and Government stores for the Eastern Arctic Patrol Service have been carried by the R.M.S. NASCOPIE which was owned and operated by the Hudson's Bay Company. More that two years ago it was decided that increasing activities in the Arctic necessitated a separate vessel for handling governmental work in this area but we are only now able to obtain the steel and other material required."

With the loss of NASCOPIE, C.G.S. N.B. McLEAN remained the only Canadian ship capable of Arctic operations until the HOWE was launched in 1950. According to the Minister, she could carry 58 crew, 58 passengers plus both dry and refrigerated cargo, "and also 30 Eskimos". One modern, and very useful touch, was a helicopter deck. A chopper not only gave her an extended reconnaissance capability for ice navigation, but also a handy way of getting people on to the beach, regardless of shore ice and surf conditions.

C.C.G.S. N.B. McLEAN

C.C.G.S. C.D. Howe

She was twin screwed, a real advantage in ice. However, with only 4,000 indicated horse power, the Howe was by no means a "heavy" icebreaker. The Americans, of course, had several, and were quite willing to send them into our North. Canada would not start building these, having 10,000 horse power or more on the shafts, until the Dew Line was under construction. Eventually, the Canadian Coast Guard would annually send up to seven heavy and two or three "medium" (4,000 s.h.p.) icebreakers into the North each season, to escort several tankers and dry cargo vessels carrying over 100,000 tons of fuel and stores to sites all over the North. This operation would be supplemented by commercial activity, ranging from oil and mineral extraction to Arctic cruising. Rather than one old coal-burning icebreaker owning the North, it was becoming a rather busy place.

A Proud Name Lives On

The proud name Nascopie lives on, both in the North and at sea. Just east of Lake Harbour on Hudson Strait is a prominence officially called Nascopie Point. Further to the west, just off Cape Dorset, the rocks she struck are now named Nascopie Reefs. The Sailing Directions describes them under "Dangers in the approaches [to Cape Dorset]"as being "composed of dangerous shoals and drying patches", not a pleasant place to have to navigate in the dark of night with incomplete charts.

On March four, 1996, the Maersk Nascopie was christened at a ceremony in St. John's. She is an offshore support vessel (O.S.V.), built to service

MAERSK NASCOPIE

the Hibernia oil platform which will be positioned 300 km to the east of that port, out in the wild North Atlantic, in the area known as "Iceberg Alley". She and her sister MAERSK NORSEMAN are fully equipped for the rugged work they have to do out there. In addition to delivering people and supplies, the two ships are equipped for fire-fighting, rescue, rig evacuation and oil-spill counter measures. Finally, they have a capability the original NASCOPIE might have envied. When a drifting iceberg threatens the platform, these ships will be able to "lasso" it and tow it aside. However, they are only strengthened for navigation in ice, not true icebreakers. One can only assume that the designer knew his Newfoundlanders and didn't want MAERSK NASCOPIE to follow her namesake to the Front to pick up a few extra bucks "swiling" in the spring.

MAERSK NASCOPIE received her name from a "name the ship" contest held for school kids across Newfoundland and Tommy Walsh, of Bay de Verte came up with the best. I guess it takes Tommy's generation to remind ours that some things still have meaning and should not be thoughtlessly cast adrift. The name NASCOPIE is one of those and, at least for people who understand Canada's historic links to the northern seas, it is satisfying to know that a new ship is sailing the rugged North Atlantic carrying the name NASCOPIE on her bows.

R.M.S. NASCOPIE

Appendix One:
Nascopie's Captains

Date	The North & Russia	Sealing
1912	A.C. Smith	
1912,13,14,15		G. Barbour
1913	J. Meikle	
1914	A.C. Smith	
1915-17	E. Mack	
1917-19	T. Smellie	
1919-21	G.H. Mead	
1921,22	L.J. Evans	
1922-25	T. Smellie	
1926	F. Walker	
1927	E. Mack	
1927,28,29,30		A. Kean
1928-30	J.W. Murray	
1933-45	T. Smellie	
1946,47	J. Waters	

Appendix Two:
Vessel Particulars

The following does not cover all of the Company's vessels, nor all vessels that went into the North. It covers only those owned or chartered by HBC and the government that are related to Nascopie's story and whose particulars are available.

Notes:

1. **IB** is a full icebreaker. **I.S.** is ice strengthened.

2. All dimensions are in metres.
   They are expressed by: length x breadth x depth x draft.

3. __ means that the data is not available.

4. **G.R.T. (Gross Registered Tons)**. This is not a measurement of weight but rather of the cubic measurement of the enclosed and watertight volume of a vessel, including engine and accommodation spaces. It is based on 100 cubic feet = one G.R.T. This formula evolved from the volume to weight of timber shipped from Quebec to Britain. Since the same vessels carry both high volume to weight cargoes such as grain, and low volume to weight ones such as iron ore, a common measurement is required to keep the owners honest. The volume of the cargo spaces only is expressed in Net Registered tons.

5. **Machinery**. Horse power (h.p.) is quoted as nominal, registered indicated or shaft. Only the last says anything really useful about what is actually delivered to the propellers. Where possible, I have made an educated guess (*). Most steam plants were either two cylinder or triple expansion, with a boiler pressure of 180 pounds per square inch (p.s.i).

6. **2 sc** = two propellers.

Name	Type	Dimensions	G.R.T.	Machinery	Builder & Date	Disposition
HBC OWNED						
Bayeskimo	steel I.S.	69.6 x 11 x 6.6 x 4.6 x ___	1391	Tr ex 97 Rhp.	Swan Hunter Tyne R., 1921	Wrecked 1922
Discovery	wood barquentine I.S.	58.8 x 11.1 x 6 x ___	751	Tr Ex 67 Rhp (* 460)	Dundee Shipbldg 1901	Sold 1912
Fort James	wood aux. schooner	33.3 x ___ x 4	96	Diesel 120 shp		
Inenew	steel	28.4 x 5.9 x 2.5 x ___	109	2 cyl. 13 Rhp	Polson Iron Works Toronto, 1902.	
Nascopie	steel IB	93.6 x 14.4 x 6.6 x 6.6	2520.2	Tr ex 339 Nhp (* 2700)	Swan Hunter Tyne R. 1911	Wrecked 1947
Pelican	wood barque I.S.	59 x 11.8 x 5.5 x ___	638	2 cyl. 122 Nhp (* 830)	Admiralty Dockyard Devonport, 1877	Sold 1922
Rupertsland	steel I.S.	56 x 10.4 x ___ x 3.3	663	Diesel 2 Sc	Fairfield Co. Glasgow, 1948	
HBC CHARTERED						
Beothic	steel IB	78.9 x 11.7 x 5.5 x ___	1140	Tr ex 328 Nhp	D.H. Henderson Glasgow, 1909	
Ungava	steel I.S.	85.7 x 14.3 x 6 x 5.9	1914	Tr ex 247 Nhp	Detroit Shipbldg, 1918	Sold 1940

Name	Type	Dimensions	G.R.T.	Machinery	Builder & Date	Disposition
GOVERNMENT (NOW CANADIAN COAST GUARD)						
Arctic	wood barquentine I.S.	54.1 x 12.1 x 6.6x __	762	Tr ex 44 Nhp	Howaldstwerke Kiel, Germany.	Sold and scrapped 1926
C.D. Howe	steel I.S.	96.7 x 16.4 x 6x __	3628	Steam unaflow 4000 Ihp 2 sc	Davie Shipbldg Lauzon, Que. 1950	Decommissioned and sold 1970
Minto	Steel IB	73.8 x 10.7 x 6.7 x__	1089	Tr ex 2900 Ihp	Gourlay Bros. Dundee 1899	Sold to Russia 1915. Wrecked
N.B. McLean	steel IB	85.2 x 19.7 x 6.6x__	3254	Tr ex 6500 Ihp 2 sc	Halifax Shipyard 1930.	Decommissioned 1979. Sold 1980
MAERSK SUPPLY SERVICES						
Maersk Nascopie	Steel offshore service I.S.	82.5 x 18.8 x 7.6 x 6.2	6740 L.D.**	2x3530 Kw Diesels (2x4800 Shp) 2 sc	Marystown Shipyard 1996	

** Since OSVs carry most of their cargo on deck, Gross Tonnage would have no application. Loaded Displacement refers to the actual weight of the vessel in the fully loaded condition at summer draft. (Some vessels are allowed to increase their draft during the good summer weather. However, they have to reduce draft, which increases freeboard, during the "Winter North Atlantic" season.)

References

As stated in the introduction, a certain amount of my material comes from what researchers call "general knowledge". In my case, that comes from both a quarter century with the Canadian Coast Guard and a lifetime of perusing countless sources, both written and verbal, on matters maritime. In addition, I have Len's general knowledge, which is much better than any book. Publications were researched however, and below are listed the main sources used specifically for this work.

The North

Anderson, W.A., *Angel of Hudson Bay,* Clarke, Erwin: Toronto, 1964

Bradbury, C., *Ten Years in the High Canadian Arctic,* R.B. Books: St. John's, 1994

Canadian Hydrographic Service *SAILING DIRECTIONS Labrador and Hudson Bay, Sixth Edition, 1988* and *Arctic Canada, Vols. One and Two, Forth Edition, 1994,* C.H.S. Ottawa

Freuchen, P., *VAGRANT VIKING My Life and Adventures,* Messner: New York, 1953

Gillis, E.M. and Myles, E., *North Pole Boarding House,* Ryerson Press: Toronto, 1951

Gray, D. and P., *The Timiskawa Navigator,* General Store Publishing House: Burnstown, 1995

National Archives of Canada. These contain some of the *Hudson's Bay Co. Archives* and *Lloyd's Register of Shipping* Ottawa

Newman, P., *Company of Adventurers,* Viking Press: Markham, 1985

Merchant Princes, Viking Press: 1993

Wild, R. *Arctic Command: The Story of Smellie of the Nascopie,* Ryerson: Toronto, 1955

Sealing

Barr, W. "S.S. Nascopie: Newfoundland Sealing Steamer," *Aspects,* Vol. 10, no. 1 (Fall, 1978) pp. 19-28

Ryan, S. (Ed), *CHAFE'S SEALING BOOK A Statisical Record of the Newfoundland Seal Fishery, 1863-1941,* Breakwater Books: St. John's, 1989

Ryan, S. SEALS AND SEALERS A Pictorial History of the Newfoundand Seal Fishery, Breakwater Books: St. John's, 1987

Ryan, S. THE ICE HUNTERS A History of Newfoundland Sealing to 1914, Breakwater Books: St. John's, 1994

Ships

Appleton, T.E. *USQUE AD MARE A History of the Canadian Coast Guard and Marine Services,* Department of Transport: Ottawa, 1968

Lloyd's Registry of Shipping, Lloyd's: London

ACKNOWLEDGEMENTS

Many people and agencies contributed in many ways to this book. Some offered anecdotes, some put me on to valuable source materials, and others provided advice and assistance. I am most grateful to all. In more concrete terms, including their names here obliges my equally grateful publisher to send them a copy of this book. We writers do earn a few perks for our efforts.

Beaver, The., Winnipeg, Manitoba
Beauchamp, R., Montreal, P.Q.
Budgell, L., Winnipeg
Canadian Coast Guard Operations Centre, Ottawa
Dillon, J., Ottawa
Hinton, C.B. Leslie, Magdalen Iles, P.Q.
Hudson's Bay Company, Winnipeg
Hudson's Bay Company Archives, Manitoba Archives, Winnipeg
Irvine, T., Ottawa
LeDrew, D. ,Cornerbrook, Nfld.
LeDrew-Keyes, B., Durham, Ont.
Millar, F.A.S. Ottawa
Murray, P.J.M., Ottawa
National Archives of Canada, Ottawa
National Library of Canada, Ottawa
Ottawa Public Library
Saunders, D. Happy Valley, Labrador
Seabase Ltd., St. John's, Nfld.
Thomson, B., St. John's, Nfld.
Walsh, T., Bay de Verte, Nfld.

PICTURE CREDITS

Beaver, The
Beauchamp, R., Montreal
Hudson Bay Company Archives
Lain Photographics Ltd., St. John's
Memorial University, St. John's
National Archives of Canada

I am on the book as author, but these fine people gave me the material that made the authoring possible. Finally, I want to thank my good wife Peg. She has always been my sternest and thus most valuable critic. Keeping this author honest is a pretty heavy go, but she uses the whip gently.

www.ingramcontent.com/pod-product-compliance
Lightning Source LLC
Chambersburg PA
CBHW070047100426
42740CB00013B/2828